College Student Outcomes Assessment:
A Talent Development Perspective

by Maryann Jacobi, Alexander Astin, and Frank Ayala, Jr.

ASHE-ERIC Higher Education Report No. 7, 1987

Prepared by

Clearinghouse on Higher Education
The George Washington University

Published by

Association for the Study of
Higher Education

Jonathan D. Fife,
Series Editor

Cite as
Jacobi, Maryann; Astin, Alexander; and Ayala, Frank, Jr., *College Student Outcomes Assessment: A Talent Development Perspective*. ASHE-ERIC Higher Education Report No. 7. Washington, D.C.: Association for the Study of Higher Education, 1987.

Managing Editor: Christopher Rigaux
Manuscript Editor: Barbara M. Fishel/Editech

The ERIC Clearinghouse on Higher Education invites individuals to submit proposals for writing monographs for the Higher Education Report series. Proposals must include:

1. A detailed manuscript proposal of not more than five pages.
2. A chapter-by-chapter outline.
3. A 75-word summary to be used by several review committees for the initial screening and rating of each proposal.
4. A vita.
5. A writing sample.

Library of Congress Catalog Card Number 88-71518
ISSN 0884-0040
ISBN 0-913317-42–X

Cover design by Michael David Brown, Rockville, Maryland

ERIC Clearinghouse on Higher Education
School of Education and Human Development
The George Washington University
One Dupont Circle, Suite 630
Washington, D.C. 20036-1183

ASHE **Association for the Study of Higher Education**
Texas A&M University
Department of Educational Administration
Harrington Education Center
College Station, Texas 77843

This publication was prepared partially with funding from the Office of Educational Research and Improvement, U.S. Department of Education, under contract no. 400-86-0017. The opinions expressed in this report do not necessarily reflect the positions or policies of OERI or the Department.

EXECUTIVE SUMMARY

Concern with outcomes assessment is by no means new in postsecondary education. Researchers, practitioners, and policy makers have long urged colleges and universities to measure the impact of their educational programs (see, for example, Bowen 1974). Recent national reports (e.g., Study Group 1984) highlight the promise and potential of outcomes assessments as tools for institutional self-improvement. But will the benefits derived from these assessments justify their costs? This monograph describes the factors that contribute to useful outcomes assessments.

A useful assessment has several distinguishing characteristics. First, the assessment produces data relevant to issues facing educational practitioners today. Second, the assessment provides information about students' change and development, not only an isolated snapshot of student competencies at a single time. Third, the longitudinal data include information about students' educational experiences so that the effects of these experiences can be assessed. Finally, the results are analyzed and presented in a manner that facilitates their use by practitioners.

Why Study Student Outcomes?

While the assessment of student outcomes has many advocates, experience has shown that such assessments often fail to live up to initial expectations about their usefulness. This gap between promise and performance often occurs because of unclear or conflicting expectations about the goals and purposes of the research. A careful consideration of the goals of assessment is essential if research methods and measures are to be matched to institutional goals and expectations. The goals of assessment may include establishing accountability for external agencies, analyzing cost effectiveness, evaluating and developing programs, setting goals, marketing, and undertaking strategic planning and basic research.

What Is Excellence?

Any attempt to implement an institutional program of assessing student outcomes should be based on some coherent *philosophy* of institutional mission. In particular, the assessment program should reflect some conception of what constitutes *effective performance* of that mission. And effective performance is of course closely allied to concepts of institutional quality or excellence.

"Excellence" and "quality" are perhaps the most fashionable terms in discussions of education these days. But even though many of us are fond of talking about excellence, we seldom take the trouble to define what we *mean* by excellence.

The two most commonly used approaches to defining excellence can be labeled as the *reputational* and *resource* approaches (Astin 1985). The reputational view holds that excellence is equated with an institution's rank in the prestige pecking order of the institution as revealed, for example, in periodic national surveys. The resource approach holds that excellence is equated with such criteria as the test scores of entering freshmen, the endowment, the physical plant, the scholarly productivity of the faculty, and so on. These approaches are mutually reinforcing in the sense that enhanced reputation can bring an institution additional resources, and additional resources like highly able students and a nationally visible faculty can enhance an institution's reputation.

Perhaps the major limitation of these traditional approaches is that they do not necessarily reflect higher education's most fundamental purpose: the education of students. If one accepts the idea that higher education's principal reason for being is to develop the talents of students, then "quality" or "excellence" should reflect *educational effectiveness* rather than mere reputation or resources. This alternative conception of excellence can be labeled the "talent development" view (Astin 1985). Under the talent development view, then, a high-quality institution is one that maximizes the intellectual and personal development of its students.

These alternative views have important implications for institutional assessment. Under the reputational and resource approaches, attention is focused on the caliber of the *entering* students as reflected in standardized admissions test scores and high school grade averages. Students who are high achievers are thus viewed as an important institutional "resource," which also tends to enhance the institution's reputation. Under a talent development approach, on the other hand, assessment focuses more on *changes* or *improvements* in students' performance from entry to exit.

How Can I Apply a Talent Development Approach on My Campus?

In actual practice, the talent development approach might be applied to an individual campus somewhat as follows: Newly admitted students would be tested to determine their entering level of competence for purposes of counseling and placement. These initial scores would be useful not only in providing information about a student's specific strengths and weaknesses but also in establishing a baseline against which to measure that student's subsequent progress. After the student completes a course of study, the same or similar assessments are repeated and the differences in performance are used in providing critical information on the student's growth and development—not only to the student but also to the professor and institution.

Outcomes assessment from a talent development perspective is characterized by longitudinal ("pretest, posttest") designs, in which a group of students are tested with the same (or comparable) measures at different times, thereby providing measures of growth and change over time. The talent development approach does not depend on the use of any particular method of assessment. Objective tests, essays, and interviews, departmental examinations, work samples, performance examinations, and any other devices might be appropriate, depending on the content and objectives of the curriculum or program being assessed.

Talent development assessments may be conducted with either standardized assessment instruments that are commercially available from testing organizations or with locally designed instruments developed by faculty and institutional researchers on campus. Standardized assessment instruments offer the user several advantages, including established reliability and validity, comparative and normative data, and efficiency in administration and analysis as a result of services from vendors. On the other hand, standardized instruments are unlikely to be useful if the testing organization and the potential user differ in the manner in which they define key concepts. Further, locally designed instruments provide an opportunity to involve faculty, administrators, staff, and students in a collaborative effort to reflect upon and define key educational objectives.

This review indicates four recurring methodological issues that influence the suitability of standardized instruments for talent development purposes: (1) the likelihood that students will bottom out or top out, thereby losing the ability to make valid longitudinal or cross-sectional comparisons; (2) the availability of item scores in addition to scale and total scores; (3) the validity of results on the individual level as well as the aggregate level; and (4) the availability of absolute rather than relativistic measures of performance. In addition, longitudinal assessments may be weakened by a variety of methodological confounds (Cook and Campbell 1979), such as the effects of maturation, instrumentation, and testing and statistical regression. Each confound reduces the likelihood that the outcomes assessment accurately measures the effect of the educational program.

This monograph also briefly describes over 25 tests that may be considered by institutions interested in assessing student outcomes. These instruments fall into three broad categories: (1) integrated packages for assessment of "general education," (2) instruments designed to assess a particular skill of importance in higher education, and (3) subject matter competency tests.

How Can I Increase the Usefulness of Outcomes Assessments on My Campus?

A successful student outcomes project not only measures impact—it also produces impact. The successful project becomes a tool for administrators, trustees, faculty, students, and external reviewers to use in evaluation and decision making. Yet all too often outcomes assessments fall short of this goal (Ewell 1983). Why are data often discounted or ignored? The monograph discusses three reasons why such assessments may fail to live up to their potential as management tools: (1) inadequate conceptualization, (2) technical barriers, and (3) political barriers.

Several aspects of the talent development perspective contribute to bridging the gap between researchers and practitioners. By rejecting an adversarial approach to evaluation in favor of an informational approach, the talent development perspective reduces defensiveness and hostility to evaluation. By emphasizing longitudinal designs with pre- and posttesting, talent development assessments reduce the ambiguity of findings; researchers and practitioners are more likely to agree on the interpretation of the results.

A review of the literature indicates a number of factors that increase the usefulness of information about outcomes:

1. Involvement of research practitioners and target audiences;
2. Support of top administrators;
3. Technical quality of the research and the interactions of technical and political issues;

4. Dissemination as an ongoing process of communication between researchers and practitioners;
5. Recommendations that are incremental and clearly connected to the data;
6. Report formats that are based on issues and directly address concerns of practitioners; and
7. Structures and settings that provide opportunities for decision makers and researchers to jointly review the data.

What Are Some Practical Suggestions For Conducting Assessments?

The monograph provides a number of practical, nuts-and-bolts suggestions for implementing a comprehensive program of outcomes assessments:

1. How to use assessments to facilitate and improve performance rather than merely to evaluate it;
2. How to build on what is already there by making better use of tests already in use;
3. How to begin development of a student data base for longitudinal student assessment;
4. How to get more from standardized tests; and
5. How to encourage students' participation in longitudinal assessments.

Is My Institution Ready to Conduct a Student Outcomes Assessment?

To assist readers in determining their readiness to implement assessment programs, a quick "self-study" guide is offered. The guide includes 15 questions for consideration in planning an assessment of outcomes and covers philosophical, conceptual, methodological, and organizational issues.

ADVISORY BOARD

CONSULTING EDITORS

Evelyn Hively
Vice President for Academic Programs
American Association of State Colleges and Universities

Frederic Jacobs
Dean of the Faculties
American University

Hans H. Jenny
Executive Vice President
Chapman College

Joseph Katz
Director, New Jersey Master Faculty Program
Woodrow Wilson National Fellowship Foundation

George Keller
Senior Vice President
The Barton-Gillet Company

L. Lee Knefelkamp
Dean, School of Education
American University

David A. Kolb
Professor and Chairman
Department of Organizational Behavior
The Weatherhead School of Management
Case Western Reserve University

Oscar T. Lenning
Executive Vice President
Dean of Academic Affairs
Waldorf College

Charles J. McClain
President
Northeast Missouri State University

Judith B. McLaughlin
Research Associate on Education and Sociology
Harvard University

Theodore J. Marchese
Vice President
American Association for Higher Education

Sheila A. Murdick
Director, National Program on Noncollegiate-Sponsored Instruction
New York State Board of Regents

Elizabeth M. Nuss
Executive Director
National Association of Student Personnel Administrators

Steven G. Olswang
Assistant Provost for Academic Affairs
University of Washington

Robert L. Payton
Scholar-in-Residence in Philanthropic Studies
University of Virginia

Henry A. Spille
Director, Office on Educational Credits and Credentials
American Council on Education

CONTENTS

FOREWORD

Student assessment is not a fad. It is not a momentary issue brought upon us by a transitory reform movement, or something that will fade away with a new administration or decade. Student assessment in one form or another has been part of higher education for years and will be with us as long as we want to know anything about the impact or effectiveness of what we are doing. The question is not why we are doing it, but rather how we can assure that the student assessment process is valid.

The higher education experience can profoundly affect a student in many ways. Intellectual growth, personal and social interactions, value and ethical development, and religious awareness are just a few of the many areas affected by college attendance. Therefore one of the major assessment issues is what is to be assessed. In this report, written by Maryann Jacobi, Alexander Astin, and Frank Ayala, Jr., the focus is on cognitive or intellectual growth or as the authors put it, "talent development." Choosing to focus on this one area is not an attempt to minimize the other effects of higher education on students; it is merely a recognition that the complexity of the issue is such that only a single-focus treatment is possible and desirable in one monograph. We fully intend to address other outcomes in future reports. The underlying reason for this focus is the great or predominant interest in assessing the intellectual outcomes of the collegiate experience.

Jacobi and Astin, both of the University of California at Los Angeles, and Ayala, of Incarnate Word College, place a special emphasis on helping the readers devise a strategy to determine whether their institutions are prepared to implement a valid assessment program. The next step in this process, of course, is to link the outcomes of this evaluation to the policy-making apparatus.

Institutions come in different sizes and shapes, public and private, teaching-oriented or research-oriented. To assume that all colleges and universities will or should instill the same values and attitudes in students is wrong and potentially harmful to parents, students, and the public alike. Assessing outcomes and being able to say "This is what our institution does" will have important implications in both faculty recruitment and student attrition rates. Knowing what your institution does *well* may be the edge needed for the next decade to come.

Jonathan D. Fife
Professor and Director
ERIC Clearinghouse on Higher Education
School of Education and Human Development
The George Washington University

ACKNOWLEDGMENTS

We have discussed issues related to the design and utilization of outcomes research with many colleagues. Their willingness to share their personal experiences with outcomes research and their insightful comments about our work have been extremely helpful in developing this monograph.

This project was supported in part by a grant from the Fund for the Improvement of Post-Secondary Education to the Higher Education Research Institute at UCLA. We especially want to acknowledge all the participants in the Value-Added Consortium. Our group meetings over the past three years have produced many stimulating discussions of outcomes research. In particular, we would like to thank FIPSE and project directors Steven Ehrmann and Russell Garth for their support. Special thanks are due as well to all those who participated in the meetings of the consortium. We would also like to acknowledge the contributions of our consultants, Trudy Banta, Peter Ewell, and Charles McClain.

Finally, special thanks are due to Jonathan Fife and Christopher Rigaux for their patience and encouragement.

GOALS OF STUDENT OUTCOMES ASSESSMENT

The assessment of student outcomes has often been advocated as a means of determining a college's success in meeting its educational goals. The assumption underlying such recommendations is that data about student outcomes indicate institutional strengths and weaknesses and thereby point to directions for improvement. This monograph discusses a variety of issues relating to the measurement of student outcomes: instruments available for such assessments, methodological challenges in measurement, and use of the resulting information.

Concern with outcomes assessment is by no means new in postsecondary education.

> *To evaluate outcomes is difficult. Yet despite these difficulties, educators have an obligation to assess outcomes as best they can, not only to appease outsiders who demand accountability, but also to improve internal management* (Bowen 1974a, p. 121).

Similarly, information about outcomes can help an institution successfully adapt to changing conditions and thereby maintain its stability and identity (Pace 1979). And a better understanding of the impacts of college on students can provide a foundation for policy development that includes educational, economic, and political considerations (Astin 1976, 1977).

The recent reports of the Study Group on the Conditions of Excellence in American Higher Education (1984) and the Association of American Colleges (AAC) (Project on Redefining 1985) highlight the promise and potential of outcomes assessments as tools for institutional self-improvement. Widespread concern about the quality of college education in the United States prompted the National Institute of Education (NIE) to convene a study group to recommend ways to improve baccalaureate education. Their final report (Study Group 1984) recommends that colleges systematically assess the development of students' knowledge, capacities, and skills during the college years. The report suggests that the results of such assessments can be used to evaluate and improve student advising and placement, curriculum development, and academic and student service programs.

> *It is futile to adjust the content and delivery of programs in accordance with redefined, detailed objectives unless one has some ways of knowing whether those adjustments have been*

Like all empirical research, outcomes assessment cannot indicate what a school's goals* should *be.

successful. A comprehensive assessment program will help faculty determine what works and what does not (Study Group 1984, p. 55).

Following the NIE and AAC reports, a number of other associations have echoed the call for research on outcomes. For example, a recent report of the National Governors Association recommends that "state attention . . . be directed to the outcomes of the higher education system—namely, measuring how much students learn in college. Assessment is a way that faculty, institutions, and institutional sponsors can focus on outcomes of students, programs, and institutions" (National Governors Association 1987, p. 156).

In response to these and other reports, a 1987 American Council on Education survey of colleges and universities in all 50 states found that 27 percent of respondents reported their states mandate assessment, with 80 percent of respondents anticipating such a situation within the next few years (El-Khawas 1987). But will the assessments undertaken by these schools really indicate what works and what does not? And will the benefits derived from these assessments justify their costs?

The answers to these questions depend on several factors. First, the assessment must produce data that are relevant to issues facing educational practitioners today. Second, the assessment should provide information about the change and development of students, not only an isolated snapshot of students' competencies at a single time. Third, the longitudinal data must include information about students' educational experiences (course-taking patterns, for example) so that the effects of these experiences can be assessed. Finally, the results must be analyzed and presented in a manner that facilitates use by practitioners.

The researcher's ability to accomplish these objectives largely depends on the manner in which outcomes are measured. The outcomes researcher must select or design a measure that defines the outcomes of interest in a manner congruent with the institution's perspectives. The measure must be sensitive to change over time and must be nested within a research design that provides comparisons across time, students, and different educational experiences. The results of measurement must be interpreted and presented in a manner that underscores their relevance to the institution's goals.

This monograph is intended to guide researchers, faculty, administrators, and policy makers in the measurement of student outcomes, providing practical suggestions to make outcomes assessments as useful as possible.

Why Study Student Outcomes?
While the assessment of student outcomes has many advocates, experience has shown that such assessments often fail to live up to initial expectations about their usefulness. This gap between promise and performance is sometimes the consequence of methodological (including measurement) shortcomings but more often occurs because of unclear or conflicting expectations about the goals and purposes of the research.

A distinction can also be made between what might be termed "active" and "passive" uses of outcomes assessment. Passive assessment, which is probably the more common application, involves the collection of a broad range of data about outcomes to enhance our understanding of how students are influenced by their educational programs and experiences. Data about outcomes collected in this manner are frequently found to have a wide range of uses in program evaluation and planning. Active outcomes assessment, on the other hand, is done with specific purposes in mind: to determine whether a particular program has its intended effects or to provide feedback for students or faculty with the specific idea of enhancing teaching and learning. Any given outcomes assessment can of course have both active and passive applications.

A careful consideration of the goals of assessment is essential if research methods and measures are to be matched to specified goals or expectations.

Establishing accountability for external agencies
Institutions of higher education receive financial and other forms of support from local, state, and federal governments, from taxpayers, from students and their families, and from a variety of foundations and organizations. The legitimacy of the institution's educational activities is established through the accreditation process, in which external reviewers evaluate the quality of various programs and curricula. The argument for institutional "accountability" is based on the assumption that institutions have a responsibility to those who provide support to demonstrate that institutional goals are being achieved in a cost-effective manner. Accountability in higher education can be defined as follows:

It means that colleges and universities are responsible for conducting their affairs so that the outcomes are worth the cost. It implies that institutional efforts would be directed toward appropriate goals and that the outcomes should be consistent with these goals and should be achieved at minimum cost. It also implies that an institution should report credible evidence on the degree to which it is achieving its mission and on its costs (Bowen 1974b, p. 1).

Research on student outcomes is only one element in a system of accountability, however (Bowen 1974b). In addition to the measurement of student outcomes, assessment for accountability could include a consideration of nonstudent outcomes, such as faculty productivity and community service. Because the primary goals of most colleges and universities concern student learning, however, the assessment of student outcomes is fundamental to assessment for accountability.

Nationwide, outcomes assessment has growing appeal as a means of establishing accountability in higher education. Approximately one-quarter of states now require state-supported institutions to provide some kind of information for assessment. While mandated assessment is necessary, however, it is not sufficient in establishing accountability.

Compared with a few years ago, . . . today assessment of student learning is no longer a foreign notion . . . . Yet what remains more elusive is the link between policies of assessment and accountability. In fewer than a dozen states are state colleges and universities required to include information on student performance assessment as a part of the documentation of institutional role and mission. Using student assessment data to improve programs, teaching, and learning, and to hold institutions accountable is also not common (National Governors Association 1987, p. 32).

The debate over the benefits and liabilities of performance-based funding and other possible consequences of state-mandated assessment is likely to continue over the next decade. In the meantime, researchers and practitioners face the challenge of designing outcomes assessments that both respond to external demands for accountability and also provide useful information for internal application.

Analysis of cost effectiveness

Closely related to assessment for accountability are analyses of cost effectiveness. While an institution might demonstrate that certain practices facilitate students' growth in desired directions, one might still ask whether the benefits accrued from these practices justify their costs. While cost effectiveness is of concern to administrators within the institution, external funding and review organizations often emphasize it.

Economists have done most of the student outcomes research by attempting to measure the economic value of a college degree for its recipients. Cost-benefit research examines short- and long-term earnings of college graduates to determine the return students receive on their investment in higher education (see, for example, Mills 1983; Solmon 1973). While much of this research is seriously flawed from the perspective of methodology, a more serious problem exists: Many, if not most, outcomes of college have a value other than monetary. A broader approach to this issue is therefore preferable; hence the term "cost-effectiveness analysis" is used instead of "cost-benefit analysis" to suggest that the costs of higher education must be weighed against the full range of monetary and nonmonetary outcomes (Rossi and Freeman 1982).

Institutional self-improvement

Assessments of outcome are useful not only for satisfying concerns about accountability of external agencies but also as an aid in planning, program development, and allocation of resources by institutional managers.

Program evaluation. Program evaluations seek to understand the particular programs and structures within the university that contribute to or detract from effectiveness. Over the past two decades, the quantity and quality of program evaluation in higher education have increased considerably, and a major distinction has been drawn between process and outcomes evaluations (cf. Rossi and Freeman 1982). Process evaluation emphasizes issues of program implementation, while outcomes evaluation is concerned with the impact of those services. A process evaluation of student counseling services, for example, might assess whether those students most needing counseling were in fact receiving the service and how much (in terms, say, of contact hours) they were receiving. An outcome evaluation of the same service, on the other hand, might assess the extent

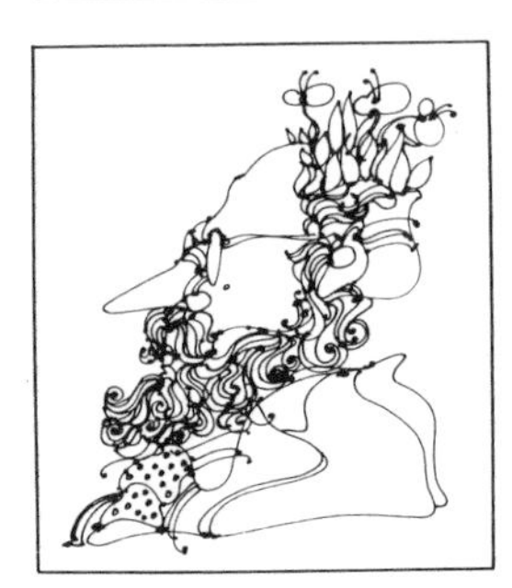

to which students' psychological or academic difficulties were resolved or ameliorated as a result of counseling. Similarly, a process evaluation of the college curriculum might focus on the types and numbers of courses taken by various students, while an outcome evaluation would look at the effect of these courses on students' cognitive skills, success at work, and so forth.

A related distinction is that between formative and summative evaluations (Sylvia, Meier, and Gunn 1985). Formative evaluations are similar to process evaluations in that they are conducted in the earlier stages of service delivery to help staff and managers be more effective in their work. Summative evaluations, on the other hand, are more like outcome evaluations in that they focus on the final impacts of the program and are more frequently used for decisions regarding future allocation of resources.

Within the framework of evaluation research, student outcome measurements are more relevant to outcome and summative evaluations than to process and formative evaluations. Process evaluations would address whether the various courses and programs were reaching the students for whom they were intended, whereas outcomes evaluations would determine whether the courses and programs were influencing student development in a manner congruent with institutional goals. Both types of evaluation information, however, could be useful to administrators facing difficult decisions about allocation of resources or to program directors seeking to develop their programs in a competitive environment.

Student services. In addition to assessing academic programs, information about outcomes can be used to improve the quality of student services. Information about student outcomes can be applied to counseling, orientation, placement, and other student personnel functions to increase the fit between students' needs and a program's impact. Within this perspective, data about outcomes are likely to be used on the individual rather than on the aggregate level. Placement tests, achievement tests, and assessments of general education represent outcomes data that can be applied to service delivery (Ewell 1983). For example, improvements shown in standardized test scores at the end of a student's freshman year could provide useful information to the student and his or her academic counselor about the student's academic needs and strengths. This information might also help identify students at risk for attrition to circumvent that possibility.

Setting goals. Assessments for accountability and evaluation as described here assume that the institution has established a set of goals and that it needs only to determine its success in meeting them. But what happens when the institution is not sure of its goals or wishes to reconsider and perhaps change them? Under these conditions, an outcomes assessment may be appropriate as well, not to evaluate progress toward some a priori set of objectives but rather to facilitate reflection upon what the school currently provides to students and how it might be improved.

When used in setting goals, outcomes assessments might focus on a broad array of student behavior, cognition, and affect and might make special efforts to discern unexpected outcomes (side effects) and negative outcomes. Qualitative approaches involving, for example, open-ended interviews with students and other constituents may prove richer and more stimulating than the traditional quantitative approaches to outcomes assessment. Obviously, as setting goals is ultimately a question of values, a student outcomes assessment will not in itself indicate what the school's goals ought to be. Rather, the assessment may serve as a starting point for discussion and reflection among students, faculty, administrators, alumni, and others about what students need to learn in college and about how the institution might best contribute to students' development. If nothing else, outcomes assessment forces us to make our implicit values and goals more explicit. And the mere process of trying to define these goals can often serve to help clarify them.

Strategic planning. Long-range, strategic planning is increasing within higher education as both a response to external demands for accountability and as a proactive effort to provide a rational basis for decision making in light of an uncertain future and rapidly changing external environment.

> *In effect, strategic planning examines the big issues—the organization's purpose, its mission, its relationship to its environment, its share of the market, its interactions with other organizations. Strategic planning is not concerned with nuts-*

and-bolts issues . . . . [It] asks the basic questions of institutional health and survival (Baldridge 1983, p. 175).

Strategic plans have five benefits: (1) to establish an organizational framework, (2) to guide delegation of responsibility and allocation of resources, (3) to help motivate people, (4) to serve as channels of communication, and (5) to provide a basis for control (or accountability) (Allen 1982).

Outcomes assessment contributes to institutional strategic planning at several stages. First, as discussed earlier, information about outcomes can assist faculty and managers within the institution in defining their goals and objectives. Similarly, data about outcomes can also point to critical issues that must be resolved for the institution to successfully achieve its goals. Third, outcomes assessments are a source of baseline data so that both student services personnel and faculty can develop programs, policies, and curricula that respond appropriately to students' needs and abilities. Finally, outcomes assessments provide essential feedback about the effectiveness of long-range plans and point to areas where plans must be modified to achieve institutional goals.

Assessment is essential in the early phases of strategic planning, necessary for the institution to identify strengths, weaknesses, and opportunities for the future (Sylvia, Meier, and Gunn 1985). Assessment for evaluative purposes is also the last stage of a strategic planning process (cf. Munitz and Wright 1980).

Other uses for information about outcomes

Marketing. An increasingly common reason for conducting outcomes assessments is to generate information that can be used to increase prospective students' awareness and understanding of the institution. In this manner, outcomes assessments become a marketing tool—a way of communicating with the community. Colleges that are trying to attract a larger pool of applicants (or trying to increase the quality or diversity of their applicants) may wish to inform selected subpopulations of prospective students about the likely outcomes of attending that school. The college may also want to educate community members about student outcomes to increase the congruence between community perceptions of the institution and the actual benefits delivered by the school.

A social marketing perspective holds that the main mission of the organization is to respond appropriately to the needs and wants of its target markets (Kotler 1982). Within this approach, outcomes assessments become a tool to determine the institution's effectiveness in meeting the goals of the community (or other target markets). For example, if certain local employers constitute one target market, the outcomes assessment might focus on those employers' ratings of the work skills of recent alumni. If the graduates of a particular high school represent another target market, the outcomes assessment might focus on the qualities most valued by those graduates (income after graduation, admissions to graduate or professional schools, employment opportunities for graduates, for example).

As competition for resources and students increases, so will strategic marketing by colleges and universities. Outcomes assessments may provide information that can be used to increase community awareness of a school, improve community attitudes, and facilitate better communication between the school and its target markets.

Basic research. Assessing the effects of college on its students is an important area of academic inquiry, even when removed from issues of immediate application to policy and management. Within the academic context, the broad area of student outcomes can be addressed from multiple levels of analysis. At the collegiate level, the researcher might explore cognitive development, social development, character development and personal growth, attitudes, values, and so forth. A broader analysis might explore the impact of college on the family, patterns of socialization, or quality of work. An even broader level of analysis might examine the impact of college on the economy, the political structure, and the culture. Academic researchers may also obtain a better understanding of the nature of colleges and universities as complex organizations by a comparison of student outcomes across diverse educational environments.

Much of the published literature on student outcomes is concerned with institutional impacts, describing, for example, the manner in which a variety of personality traits and attitudes change during the college years (Bowen 1980; Feldman and Newcomb 1969). Such information is probably not perceived as especially helpful by administrators struggling to allocate resources, define policy, or develop programs to facilitate the development of students. Nonetheless, such information does provide a backdrop against which to interpret observed outcomes within a single institution at one time. The academic perspective also makes us step back from day-to-day decisions to observe some major impacts of a college education that might otherwise go unnoticed. In this manner, data without immediate applications may prove useful over time.

Problems in the Use of Data about Outcomes

Although outcomes information can contribute to both accountability assessments and institutional self-improvement, many institutional researchers have found that their reports on outcomes only collect dust. Despite their potential as useful management tools, the data are often discounted or ignored. The assessment of student outcomes can in no way be cost effective if managers, faculty, or other practitioners do not use the results. Obstacles to use come in four broad categories.

First, outcomes assessments may fail to live up to their potential as management tools as a result of inadequate conceptualization. A careful consideration of the purposes of assessment is essential if research methods and procedures are to be matched to specified goals or expectations. For example, a project that is intended to facilitate reflection upon institutional goals or curriculum by faculty members may look quite different from one that is intended to satisfy concerns of a state government about accountability. The objectives of the outcomes assessment will influence decisions regarding methodology, instrumentation, analysis, report format, and dissemination. The successful project will be based on a set of objectives that is clearly delineated and shared by researchers and decision makers.

A second reason for underuse of information about outcomes is technical barriers. Methodology that fails to eliminate major competing hypotheses, instruments that lack established reliability or validity, errors in analysis, and so forth significantly reduce the ability of an assessment to accurately and unambiguously point to major outcomes. For example, many outcomes projects use cross-sectional rather than longitudinal designs, and others neglect to include comparison groups. Another more common deficiency is the failure to include "environmental" information about the students' educational experiences (Astin and Ayala 1987). Such common approaches are technically unsuited to determining the effects of college experiences on students' development.

Third, outcomes research is neglected or discounted as the result of political barriers. Outcomes research is one of many pieces of information available to practitioners about institutional performance. Many other sources of data are available to administrators, including subjective impressions, informal interactions, committee reports and recommendations, reports by external agencies, and institutional ratings or reputation (Weiss 1988). Thus, research data must compete with many other sources of information to influence policy decisions.

Further, many postsecondary institutions are highly conservative and faculty or administrators may be invested in maintaining the status quo. Under such circumstances, resistance is mobilized when change is recommended, and information about outcomes may become a victim of academic gamesmanship (Astin 1976).

Political barriers often masquerade as technical barriers to use. For example, practitioners who find that empirical findings threaten the status quo may choose to criticize research methodology rather than take issue directly with the research findings. This event is particularly likely when faculty members are asked to play an active role in applying data about outcomes to modifications in program or policy. The situation can also be reversed so that technical barriers may appear at first glance to be political barriers. For example, a poorly written research report may discourage active consideration by practitioners, or an inappropriate analysis may produce data that are irrelevant to institutional issues and therefore ignored.

Finally, outcomes research will be underused if it is commissioned to indicate the "best" outcomes or directions for the institution. Like all empirical research, outcomes assessments cannot indicate what a school's goals *should* be (Baird 1976; Bowen 1974b). Although outcomes research can provide an accurate description of how students change in response to college, the value attached to these changes is ultimately subjective and cannot be empirically determined (Astin 1970). Facilitation of one outcome may mean that another is overlooked; outcomes research cannot indicate which tradeoffs are most appropriate for a given institution. Nor can it tell if the costs of providing certain student services or educational programs are justified by the value of the outcomes they facilitate.

Scope of the Analysis

Information about student outcomes can play a critical role in institutional planning and policy development; however, the measurement of student outcomes poses numerous technical and political challenges. Additional challenges are incurred in designing assessments that can be applied to institutional management and decision making.

The rewards of well-planned student outcomes assessments justify their cost, however. The goal of this monograph is to increase the usefulness of research on outcomes by offering solutions to some of the challenges practitioners frequently encounter in gathering information about outcomes or in conducting research about outcomes. Issues of measurement are emphasized, as little information is currently available about this critical component of research about outcomes. The following sections review available instruments for the measurement of student outcomes, offer solutions to some methodological problems, and discuss the relationship between measurement and use of information about outcomes.

Selection of measurement methods and instruments is always based on some implicit or explicit theory of student outcomes. When underlying beliefs are unexamined and implicit, selected measures may ultimately prove inappropriate for institutional goals and policy making. Reflection and discussion about different concepts of student outcomes, in contrast, will increase the likelihood that subsequent research will be useful to administrators.

The following sections discuss three broad areas of concern in conducting useful assessments of outcome: (1) philosophical and conceptual issues, (2) measurement issues, and (3) contextual issues related to the integration of research into institutional decision making. The next section describes a philosophy of institutional excellence and effective performance called "talent development" (Astin 1985) and suggests that talent development provides a useful framework to plan, administer, interpret, and apply information about student outcomes. The third section provides a more concrete discussion of conceptual issues by reviewing outcomes taxonomies that may guide institutions in identifying critical student outcomes. After determining the factors to assess, the selection of appropriate measurement tools poses many challenges. The fourth section offers a general discussion of issues to consider in the selection or design of measurement instruments, and the fifth reviews over 25 cognitive assessment instruments that may be considered for use within a talent development perspective. The sixth and seventh sections focus on contextual issues, with the sixth providing a review of evaluation literature related to the use of research findings and the seventh offering a number of practical suggestions to help institutions get started in assessment from a talent development perspective.

The following sections, and especially the fourth and fifth ones, tend to emphasize cognitive rather than affective outcomes. In part, the focus on cognitive outcomes is to fill a gap in the literature. A considerable volume of research, extending over two decades, addresses affective outcomes of higher education (see, for example, Astin 1977; Feldman and Newcomb 1969; Pace 1979). Cognitive outcomes, however, have not received this attention in the literature. Thus, the assessment of cognitive outcomes, which is perhaps the most difficult task associated with assessment, deserves extra attention and visibility.

A secondary reason for this focus is that cognitive outcomes are central to the mission of higher education and increasingly a concern of the educational reform movement.

> *Assessment of undergraduate learning and college quality needs, at minimum, to include data about student skills, abilities, and cognitive learning; substantive knowledge of individual students and groups of students at various points in their undergraduate careers; instructional approaches used by faculty; and educational curricula* (National Governors Association 1986, p. 156).

Thus, increasing numbers of practitioners and administrators are likely to face both external and internal demands for information about cognitive outcomes. Many of the conceptual and empirical issues discussed in this monograph, however, are likely as applicable to affective as well as to cognitive outcomes and will be helpful to those readers with interests in a broad array of outcomes.

A PHILOSOPHY OF ASSESSMENT

Any attempt to implement an institutional program of assessing student outcomes should be based on some coherent *philosophy* of institutional mission. In particular, the assessment program should reflect some conception of what constitutes *effective performance* of that mission. Effective performance, of course, is closely allied to concepts of institutional quality or excellence. This section first discusses the authors' conception of institutional quality or excellence and then suggests some theoretical and philosophical perspectives that might be applied in developing a program of institutional outcomes assessment.

Perhaps the major limitation of these traditional approaches [to defining excellence] is that they do not necessarily reflect higher education's most fundamental purpose: The education of students.

What Is "Excellence"?

"Excellence" and "quality" are perhaps the most fashionable terms in discussions of education these days. But even though many of us are fond of talking about excellence, we seldom take the trouble to define what we mean by excellence in the first place, which is not to say that there are no certain implied definitions underlying many of the time-honored practices of institutional assessment. What we have failed to do is to make these definitions more explicit and to examine them critically.

The two most commonly used approaches to defining excellence can be labeled as the *reputational* and *resource* approaches (Astin 1985). The reputational view holds that excellence is equated with an institution's rank in the prestige pecking order of the institution as revealed, for example, in periodic national surveys. The resource approach holds that excellence is equated with such criteria as test scores of entering freshmen, the endowment, the physical plant, the scholarly productivity of the faculty, and so on. These approaches are mutually reinforcing in the sense that enhanced reputation can bring an institution additional resources, and additional resources like highly able students and a nationally visible faculty can enhance an institution's reputation.

Perhaps the major limitation of these traditional approaches is that they do not necessarily reflect higher education's most fundamental purpose: The education of students. If one accepts the idea that higher education's principal reason for being is to develop the talents of students—or, as the economists would say, to develop the "human capital" of the nation—then "quality" or "excellence" should reflect *educational effectiveness* rather than mere reputation or resources. This alternative conception of excellence can be labeled the "talent development" view (Astin 1985). The talent development view, then, holds that a high-quality institution is one that maximizes the intellectual and personal development of its students.

These alternative views have important implications for institutional assessment. Under the reputational and resource approaches, attention is focused on the caliber of *entering* students as reflected in standardized admissions test scores and high school grade averages. High-achieving students are thus viewed as an important institutional "resource" that also tends to enhance the institution's reputation. Under a talent development approach, on the other hand, assessment focuses more on *changes* or *improvements* in students' performance from entry to exit.

In actual practice, the talent development approach might be applied to an individual campus somewhat as follows. Newly admitted students would be tested to determine their entering level of competence for purposes of counseling and placement. These initial scores would be useful not only in providing information about a student's specific strengths and weaknesses but also in establishing a baseline against which to measure that student's subsequent progress. After the student completes a course of study, the same or similar assessments are repeated and the differences in performance used in providing critical information about the student's growth and development—not only to the student but also to the professor and institution.

The talent development approach does not depend on the use of any particular method of assessment. Objective tests and essays, interviews, departmental examinations, work samples, performance examinations, and any other devices might be appropriate, depending on the content and objectives of the curriculum or program being assessed.

A Theory of Educational Practice

How can talent development assessment be used to improve educational practices? To answer this question, it is first necessary to outline at least the basic elements of the authors' conception of how administrators and faculty members operate and how students learn and develop.

The educational practitioner is a kind of "performing artist" (Astin and Scherrei 1980). Following this analogy, it is important to realize that an essential ingredient in any performing artist's development of technique and skills is the opportunity to view the results of his or her work. Neophyte painters see what comes out on the canvas, and aspiring musicians hear what they play or sing—and they adjust their behavior accordingly.

If administrators and faculty members try to enhance the student's talent development as a means of gauging the effectiveness of their efforts, it seems that few of these practitioners ever receive appropriate feedback about the results of their practices. They are like artists learning to paint blindfolded or musicians learning to play the violin with their ears plugged.

While it is true that college faculty members, as they practice the "performing art" of teaching and learning, receive some informal feedback from their students, this input rarely provides any systematic information about how much and how well students are actually learning. Professors might argue that their final examinations allow them to evaluate the quality of learning, but in many respects, relying on final examinations is like closing the barn door after the horse has escaped. Indeed, performance on final examinations is very difficult to evaluate without some clear notion as to how well students were performing at the beginning of the course. As for advising, professors rarely have the opportunity to learn about their success and failures in this important enterprise.

The analogy of performing artist can be extended to support staff as well. Many areas of institutional functioning affect students directly: registration, orientation, financial aid, housing, food services, parking, social activities, career counseling, personal counseling, extracurricular activities, health services, job placement. How can the personnel responsible for these diverse student services improve their programs and policies unless they solicit systematic evaluations of their efforts from the students they serve?

What kinds of information about student development are most likely to be of use to faculty and administrators? If these practitioners are to develop effective short- and long-term strategies for their colleges and students, they must have a theory of how students learn, of what facilitates or inhibits students' educational development. While each institution must develop its own theory, *some* theory is a critical ingredient in designing a truly effective assessment program. The authors' preference is for a theory of student development that has evolved from several major studies of institutional impact on student development (see Astin 1975, 1977, 1985). A principal concept in this theory is that of *student involvement*, the time and the physical and psychological energy that the student invests in the academic experience. The more students are involved in the academic experience, the greater their learning and growth and the more fully their talents are likely to develop. The less they are involved, the less they learn and the greater the chances they will become dissatisfied and drop out. Under these circumstances, talent development is obviously minimized. A recent report, *Involvement in Learning: Realizing the Potential of American Higher Education* (Study Group 1984), embraces the involvement theory. The concept of involvement suggests, among other things, that any assessment program should attempt to determine how much time and energy students actually invest in their educational experience.

OUTCOME TAXONOMIES

This monograph offers a broad definition of student outcomes as "the wide range of phenomena that can be influenced by the educational experience." While such a definition has the advantage of allowing practitioners to interpret talent development assessments in the manner that best fits their needs, it leaves a number of questions unanswered. For example, what behaviors, cognitions, and attitudes is the educational program designed to enhance? Can we observe outcomes of college while the college experience is still unfolding (that is, while students are still enrolled), or must we wait until many years after graduation? Should outcomes be limited to the effects of the formal educational program, or should we also examine the often serendipitous results of informal experiences? Is it appropriate to limit our assessments to the planned or expected effects of a program, or should we also examine possible unintended "side effects"?

Taxonomies provide a menu from which researchers and practitioners may select the items of greatest importance to measure and track.

The authors' definition should also be viewed in light of whether outcomes assessment is an exercise in *description* or in *explanation*. Research on outcomes can attempt to establish causal relationships between the college environment and observed student outcomes, or it can merely document students' performance at particular points in time. By focusing on outcomes that can be influenced by the educational programs, the authors' definition clearly reflects a concern with the impact of the college environment on students.

In implementing a talent development philosophy and assessment program, faculty, staff, and managers must carefully consider the outcomes of most importance to the mission and goals of the institution. Efforts to identify appropriate outcome measures can be aided by a variety of outcome taxonomies. Perhaps the most important contribution of such taxonomies to implementation of a talent development approach is to support institutional dialogue about the outcomes of most importance to a college or university. From this perspective, taxonomies provide a menu from which researchers and practitioners may select the items of greatest importance to measure and track.

This chapter describes four different outcome taxonomies, each of which has been widely used in institutional planning and research. Three of them (Lenning, Bowen, and Astin) were developed from relatively global or broad perspectives, providing a comprehensive set of potential outcomes. The fourth was developed by faculty, institutional researchers, and administrators in response to the goals and mission of a particular institution, Alverno College. Because these taxonomies differ in content, organization, and breadth, they are best viewed as complementary rather than competing schemas.

Lenning

Lenning and associates (1977, 1980) present a highly refined and detailed taxonomy of outcomes. In traditional taxonomic style, they offer several major headings, each of which includes various levels and types of outcomes. Major categories of outcomes include, first, *economic outcomes*, including students' access to resources, accumulation of resources, production, and so forth. Economic resource outcomes emphasize the contribution of higher education to an individual's future income, earning ability, and productivity. A second category Lenning proposes is *human characteristics outcomes.* This somewhat generalized phrase subsumes such outcomes as aspirations, competence and skills, morale, personality, physical/physiological characteristics, social activities, and social status and recognition. The third category, *knowledge, technology, and art form functions,* includes those outcomes most directly linked to substantive elements of college education, such as general and specialized knowledge, research and scholarship products, and art works. *Resource and service provision outcomes,* the fourth category, includes the provision of facilities, events, and services. The final category comprises *aesthetic and cultural activities* as well as the organization and operation of the institution.

Lenning's typology, which was derived from a content analysis of the literature on outcomes, is most distinctive for its comprehensive detail. (In fact, his typology is not restricted only to student outcomes, and the last two categories described in the preceding paragraph are focused on the organizational or community level of analysis.) Lenning's approach is most congruent with a management perspective, as the typology delineates a range of outcomes that can serve as evaluation criteria and guide decision makers in allocating resources (Ewell 1983).

The broad range of outcomes Lenning describes may suggest to researchers that an outcomes assessment should include an equally broad range of dependent variables. While this approach may be appropriate under certain circumstances, the most useful assessments will be based on outcomes that have been carefully selected for their relevance to institutional goals and policy questions.

Bowen

Like Lenning, Bowen (1980) offers a taxonomic system that is based on a review and content analysis of the literature on student outcomes and includes outcomes at levels of analysis other than the individual student. In contrast to Lenning, however, Bowen ties his typology to goals that many institutions hold for their students. In fact, he offers a catalog of goals rather than outcomes and then uses this catalog to organize his review of the literature on student outcomes. This organizational system may be directly translated into research objectives, as the selection of dependent variables is clearly linked to institutional goals.

Bowen's five main categories are *cognitive learning, emotional and moral development, practical competence, direct satisfactions from college,* and the *avoidance of negative outcomes*. The content of Bowen's schema differs from Lenning's in several ways. First, Bowen includes a more detailed list of outcomes of practical competence, while Lenning includes more outcomes involving human characteristics. Second, Bowen emphasizes the avoidance of negative outcomes, which can add an additional dimension to assessments of outcome (similar to side effects in medical research). Third, Bowen includes students' satisfaction with college as a major classification of outcomes.

Astin

Like Bowen's, Astin's taxonomy (1974, 1977) is driven by a consideration of the goals of higher education, which includes faculty development and community services as well as student outcomes. (This discussion, however, is limited to student outcomes.) Astin's taxonomy is more complex than Lenning's and Bowen's in the sense that it includes three dimensions: type of outcome, type of data, and time. Further, Astin provides a taxonomic system for *measures* of student outcomes, while Lenning and Bowen classify outcome *variables*.

The type of outcome is divided into cognitive and affective:

> *Cognitive measures have to do with behavior that requires the use of high-order mental processes, such as reasoning and logic . . . . Noncognitive, or affective, measures have to do with the student's attitudes, values, self-concept, aspira-*

tions, and social and interpersonal relationships (Astin 1974, p. 30).

Type of data refers to the manner in which each outcome is actually measured. "Psychological" measures reflect the internal states of individuals, while "behavioral" measures refer to their observable activities.

Astin's third dimension is time. Some outcomes of college are observable after a brief period of time and may be measurable while the individual is still a student. Others may not be observable or measurable for many years. For example, students' knowledge of current research findings within their major field is a short-term outcome that can be measured after several semesters or classes. In contrast, students' ability to effectively apply this knowledge in their chosen careers is a long-term outcome that cannot be assessed until after the student has held a career position for some time.

Compared to Lenning and Bowen, Astin provides less detail about specific student outcomes. Because Astin argues, however, that a comprehensive outcomes assessment requires all eight types of data (2 × 2 × 2), his three-way matrix can provide a basis for evaluating available outcome data. For example, one might discover that some institutions collect data almost exclusively within one or two cells of the matrix and thereby obtain an incomplete picture of student outcomes. Other schools might have data available from all cells but might require more depth and detail within a single cell or better integration across cells.

Mentkowski and Doherty

One distinguishing aspect of Mentkowski and Doherty's taxonomic system (1983) is that it was collaboratively developed by faculty and administrators at Alverno College as an integral element of their efforts to implement an "outcome-centered liberal arts program." The other taxonomies described here were developed as part of scholarly research rather than as part of institutional management and decision making.

In response to increasing concerns about institutional accountability and changing needs of students, Alverno College decided to implement an outcome-centered liberal arts program in 1973. The faculty was asked to identify broad educational goals and to suggest how those goals could be defined, assessed, and validated. Students' progress toward the goals was measured at several points, both during and after college.

Faculty identified eight outcomes for assessment that reflected their views about the goals of the liberal arts program: *communications, analysis, problem solving, valuing, social interaction, taking responsibility for the environment, involvement in the contemporary world*, and *aesthetic response*. This broad taxonomy of outcomes became the basis for student assessments and evaluations of educational effectiveness.

Unlike the taxonomies previously presented, the Alverno taxonomy was developed in concert with a reconceptualization of the institution's goals. Lenning's, Bowen's, and Astin's taxonomies, in contrast, were derived from an analysis of the literature on student outcomes. The Alverno outcomes, however, cluster heavily in Lenning's "human characteristics" category. They appear to be somewhat more dispersed across Bowen's categories, covering "cognitive learning," "emotional and moral development," and "practical competence." Viewed from Astin's perspective, the Alverno model includes both affective and cognitive outcomes, both behavioral and psychological data, and assessments conducted at several points in time.

The advantage of the Alverno taxonomy is that it is highly congruent with the goals of the institution. Because the taxonomy was developed internally, key decision makers perceived it as valid and relevant. As a result, program evaluations and outcomes assessments derived from the taxonomy have become integral aspects of institutional management. One political disadvantage of this taxonomy is that it is restricted to those outcomes viewed as most important by the community. Consequently, research based solely on these eight categories may overlook outcomes that are potentially important from alternative perspectives.

The following discussion emphasizes cognitive outcomes of postsecondary education. Cognitive outcomes are typically perceived as the most important college outcomes and most related to primary goals of the institution. A broad range of constituents and decision makers within the institution share a concern with students' cognitive development as a result of their college education. Therefore, cognitive outcome assessments are most likely to gain acceptance from institutional leaders. A second reason for the emphasis on cognitive outcomes is that those who argue for greater "accountability" in higher education typically have cognitive outcomes in mind.

The assessment of cognitive outcomes of college is a challenging task. The following sections consider in depth both the technical and political problems such projects may encounter and offer guidelines to the solution of such problems.

ISSUES OF MEASUREMENT IN TALENT DEVELOPMENT ASSESSMENT

An institution embarking on a talent development assessment must face the challenge of selecting or devising appropriate assessment instruments. This section discusses some broad methodological issues to consider in selecting an appropriate measurement instrument.

The discussion of measurement issues focuses on the assessment of cognitive outcomes. While a talent development approach can (and should) include affective as well as cognitive outcomes, the measurement of cognitive outcomes is especially difficult. Researchers interested in assessing affective outcomes can choose between several widely used instruments (for example, the Cooperative Institutional Research Program Freshman and Follow-up Surveys, the College Student Experiences Questionnaire developed by C. Robert Pace), but researchers interested in assessing cognitive outcomes will encounter considerable confusion about the appropriate instruments. Focusing the discussion on cognitive instruments has the aim of reducing this confusion, with the added hope that the issues discussed may prove helpful in planning affective, attitudinal, and behavioral outcomes assessments as well.

Any college that has not thought carefully about the operational definitions of its high-priority outcomes is not ready to select and administer standardized assessments.

Finding the Instrument to Fit the Institution's Needs

Talent development assessments may be conducted with standardized assessment instruments, commercially available from testing organizations, or with locally designed instruments developed by faculty and institutional researchers on campus. Standardized assessment instruments offer the user several advantages relative to instruments designed within the institution. First, these measures generally have established reliability and validity. Second, comparative and normative data based on national samples of students are often available and can be useful in the interpretation of test results. Finally, such instruments are usually more efficient to administer and score, given the established procedures and support services provided by the vendors.

Even with these advantages, institutions often find established instruments unsuited to their needs. Of primary concern is the fit between how testing organizations and institutional personnel define key concepts for assessment. Concepts such as analytical abilities, problem solving, critical thinking, and writing ability are subject to a wide range of interpretation. If the institution's leaders (be they academic officers or faculty researchers) and the test vendors differ in their conceptual definitions and interpretations, the established instrument is unlikely to be useful to the institution, despite its technical strengths.

An even greater danger is using standardized instruments to *avoid* internal efforts to clarify key concepts or to define goal statements. By accepting without reflection a concept or definition offered by a vendor, an institution loses (or at best defers) an important opportunity to reflect on educational goals and objectives. As a result, both practitioners and researchers are likely to find that the information collected fails to inform evaluation or program and curriculum development. According to Ernest L. Boyer, "Any college that has not thought carefully about goals should not even open the issue of collegewide assessment" (*Chronicle of Higher Education* 15 October 1986, p. 41). To this might be added that any college that has not thought carefully about the operational definitions of its high-priority outcomes is not ready to select and administer standardized assessments.

Several researchers and practitioners have argued that standardized tests that measure meaningful outcomes of higher education are simply unavailable.

> *Thus, there are standardized tests available that seek to measure achievement in both general and specialized education. But for the most part, the tests are, we believe, restricted. . . . Colleges run the risk of measuring that which matters least* (Boyer 1987, p. 256).

Standardized tests focus on minimum competence rather than advanced knowledge and emphasize specialized knowledge over more abstract but more important outcomes (Edgarton 1987). Similarly,

> *When the objectives for a general education curriculum are compared with the content of the commercial tests available, it is apparent that none of the tests measure more than half of the broad understanding most faculty members believe general education should impart* (Banta and Fisher 1987, p. 45).

Recent innovative approaches to test design, however, indicate a growing interest among vendors and researchers in the development of instruments that respond to institutional needs. For example, the ETS Academic Profile, now being pilot tested, is designed to measure students' skills within broad academic areas, not specialized knowledge. Other efforts to design standardized writing assessments are useful, fair, and affordable (Quellmalz 1984).

Even when an instrument does appear to match the needs of the institution, difficulties may arise in relationships with vendors. Institutional researchers should discuss their goals for assessment and research design with vendors so that they can determine in advance whether vendors will provide support for talent development. When vendors resist applications of existing instruments for talent development (for example, by providing only total scores rather than item or subscale scores or by providing only relativistic rather than absolute scores), groups of institutions making joint appeals are likely to be more effective than individual requests for accommodation.

In contrast, locally developed assessment instruments can respond directly to institutional goals and priorities. They provide an opportunity to involve faculty and managers in a collaborative effort to reflect upon and define key educational objectives. As a result, a number of outcomes researchers strongly support the use of locally developed instruments.

> *In general, then, if one wishes to reach a specific decision, it is better to use a locally devised questionnaire concerning specific local conditions or to adapt an instrument from another institution than to use a device developed for a broad, national market that can focus only on general questions. One may lose national comparative information, but one increases the direct applicability of results* (Baird 1976, p. 17).

Nonetheless, locally developed assessments have several disadvantages. First, they are expensive and time consuming to develop. Second, they may lack established test-retest reliability, internal consistency, and validity, therefore yielding results of questionable accuracy. Third, comparative data from other institutions are rarely available for locally developed instruments, and longitudinal data providing trends over time may be similarly unavailable. The absence of cross-sectional or longitudinal comparisons may limit one's ability to clearly interpet the data collected and develop action recommendations on the basis of the findings.

To minimize the tradeoffs between standardized and locally developed instruments, institutions should consider using both approaches in combination, thereby providing multiple measures of key outcomes. Although any single instrument may be insufficient to assess key outcomes when used alone, standardized tests can significantly contribute to an understanding of students' learning, especially when used in combination with other instruments and approaches. Institutions with vigorous value-added assessment programs in place, such as Alverno College and Northeast Missouri State University, tend to use a combination of standardized tests and surveys as well as locally designed assessment tools.

Methodological Issues for Consideration in Selecting Assessment Instruments

The review of cognitive assessment instruments indicates four recurring methodological issues that influence the suitability of quantitative instruments for talent development purposes. Consideration of these issues is essential in selecting or developing assessment tools.

First is the likelihood that students will bottom out on the pretest or top out on the posttest. If a test is too hard or too easy for a group, researchers will lose the ability to make valid cross-sectional and longitudinal comparisons. For example, although an incoming freshman cohort may demonstrate a range of scores on many basic skills tests, graduating seniors may tend to top out, limiting the worth of a talent development assessment approach. On the other hand, some subject matter competency tests may prove of such difficulty to freshmen that their scores would show little variance.

The psychological effects of bottoming out on a pretest also deserve consideration. An unanticipated effect of pretesting under these conditions may be anxiety, discouragement, frustration, and anger among students who have struggled for several hours with questions that are beyond their current capabilities. These negative effects may be particularly acute when such tests are administered to incoming freshmen, many of whom are already uncertain about their ability to succeed in the new, more demanding college environment. A related concern, called "evaluation apprehension" (Cook and Campbell 1979) refers to the common desire to be evaluated favorably by researchers. Students' inability to achieve this goal may be distressing and lead to increased levels of test anxiety in the future.

A second methodological factor for consideration in the selection of standardized tests is the provision of item scores as well as scaled and total scores. An item-by-item analysis most appropriately serves the diagnostic and evaluation purposes of a talent development approach. For example, an individual student may receive similar total or scaled scores on a pre- and a posttest; however, an item analysis could show that scores in one area increased significantly while those in another section decreased. In addition, item-by-item analyses provide an opportunity to determine more precisely the level of knowledge or skill achieved by a cohort of students. Unfortunately, many commercially available instruments, such as the SAT and the GRE, do not provide item scores, limiting the usefulness of the test for talent development applications.

The third methodological issue involves the validity of individual rather than aggregate scores. Several of the instruments to be reviewed, such as the ACT COMP Objective Test, provide scores that are meaningful only for a cohort. While such aggregate analyses can be helpful in gauging the progress of groups of students, institutions also need pretest scores for the academic placement and diagnosis of individual students. In this case, users should carefully review measures for the reliability of individual scores. With aggregate scores, one must be aware of the potential threat to validity posed by significant attrition from the sample assessed. In such instances, an appropriate response would involve recalculation of pretest scores based on the sample completing the posttest. By being alert to such issues, an institution's talent development efforts will clearly benefit.

A fourth issue is the need for absolute measures as well as relativistic measures. Test scores that reflect a student's performance relative to other students pose difficulties in longitudinal repeated-measures assessments designed to indicate students' development. For example, relativistic scores often mask improvements in a student's test performance, because the total cohort may show similar (or greater) increases. Selective attrition from a sample can further reduce the usefulness of relative scores as indicators of talent development, as characteristics of the groups against which an individual's performance is evaluated or ranked may change significantly between pretest and posttest.

Confounding Factors in the Administration Of Pre- and Posttest Assessments

A useful program for assessment adheres to established standards of research design (see Astin 1970; Cook and Campbell 1979; and Kerlinger 1973 for in-depth discussions of research design for outcomes assessment). It should be noted, however, that assessment findings are uninterpretable in the absence of comparison groups. What does it mean, for example, to find that students gained 60 points on a standard test of cognitive ability between their freshman and senior years? The data have more relevance when one compares, for example, social science to physical science majors or on-campus residents to commuting students. Even under these conditions, however, the effects of the particular institutional environment on students' development cannot be discerned, because the study provides no variation on this dimension. For this reason, multi-institutional studies, despite the logistical problems they can present, are strongly recommended.

The selection of a standardized instrument for talent development assessment must be guided not only by the manner in which the test defines key concepts but also by such test characteristics as internal reliability, test-retest reliability, and convergent and discriminant validity. Even when standardized instruments have established reliability and validity, however, the manner in which such instruments are administered in the field is of critical importance to the accuracy of the findings. A variety of threats can affect the internal, construct, and external validity of applied research (Cook and Campbell 1979). Threats to the validity of pre- and posttest assessments provide alternative explanations for observed changes in students' scores, thereby raising the possibility that such changes are an artifact of uncontrolled factors rather than the result of the educational program. This section briefly describes the potential confounds of most relevance to outcomes assessment in higher education.

History

History can be a threat "when an observed effect might be due to an event that [takes] place between the pretest and the posttest, when this event is not the treatment of research interest" (Cook and Campbell 1979, p. 51). Outcomes assessments are particularly vulnerable to this threat, especially when a considerable period of time elapses between pretest and posttest. For example, an international event that captures students' involvement or a summer tour to Europe for a group of students may lead to a gain in scores on political science measures that are independent of the effects of the curriculum. Alternatively, a major concert on campus attended by large numbers of students the night before the posttest may lead to tired students and depressed scores the following day. Under these circumstances, historical factors provide alternative explanations for an observed change from pretest to posttest. If these factors are not taken into account, practitioners may draw misleading conclusions from the data.

Maturation

When changes from pre- to posttest are potentially the effect of simple development rather than an educational intervention, maturation may be a confounding factor. Maturation is the major confounding variable in value-added assessments (Pascarella 1987). The possible solution to this confound of providing comparison groups of young adults who are not enrolled in college presents both practical problems (securing compliance from such a group and finding the resources internally to support this effort) and technical problems (because youth who do attend and who do not attend college differ in many ways). Comparing changes in scores of traditional 18- to 22-year-old students with those of older, returning students can also be a means of identifying the possible effects of maturation (Pascarella 1987).

Testing

Multiple administrations of the same test may improve students' performance as a result of the effect of practice. For talent development assessments, this confound is likely when tests are administered within a relatively short time and/or at repeated points. Vendors that offer alternative, parallel forms of the same instrument provide one method of avoiding this confound.

Instrumentation

Instrumentation threatens validity when observed changes from pre- to posttest may be the result of a change in the measuring instrument, an especially likely possibility when the "measuring instrument" is human. For example, if a team of faculty members is asked to review students' essays to measure the development of writing abilities over time, findings may be confounded by systematic variations in the review process between the pre- and posttest (or even within a test session, if different reviewers are inconsistent). Similarly, different styles of administering the pre- and posttest (for example, providing extra time or helpful hints) may lead to instrumentation confounds. Using standardized, detailed criteria for the administration and scoring of tests, with frequent inter-rater reliability checks, is one way to reduce the threat of instrumentation. Another approach is to review both pretests and posttests at the same time or to reread a sample of pretests following administration of the posttests to determine whether grading criteria are being applied in a similar manner.

Instrumentation is also a potential threat if different forms of established instruments are not equivalent. Although most testing companies establish the equivalence of alternative forms of the same test according to a rigorous set of standards, review of this methodology by faculty with expertise in testing and assessment can serve to reassure others within the institution that alternative test forms are indeed parallel. Instrumentation may also be a problem when test vendors regularly update tests and then retire older versions. Should such turnover occur between a pre- and a posttest, the equivalence of the examinations may be questionable.

A related confounding factor, classified as a threat to construct validity (Cook and Campbell 1979) is the experimenter's expectancies. That is, researchers' expectations can become self-fulfilling prophecies. Within higher education, this phenomenon may be a particular concern when faculty are asked to rate students' development in those disciplines in which they teach. Under these conditions, the effects of the experimenter's expectancies can be reduced by procedures that "blind" faculty to the characteristics of the student or test (for example, by not informing faculty if the examination under review is a pretest or a posttest or if the examinee is a freshman or a senior).

Statistical regression

Statistical regression is a threat when scores at extremes of a scale are unstable. It is of particular concern in talent development assessments when students are classified into groups on the basis of pretest scores. Statistical regression:

> *(1) operates to increase obtained pretest-posttest gain scores among low pretest scores, . . . (2) operates to decrease ob-*

tained change scores among persons with high pretest scores . . . , and (3) does not affect observed change scores among scorers at the center of the pretest distribution (Cook and Campbell 1979, pp. 52–53).

This problem can be corrected by using residual gain scores derived from regression analysis instead of raw change scores (Astin 1970). Although statistical regression can be reduced by selecting instruments with high test-retest reliability, it should be of some concern in any assessment program that focuses on students with extremely high or extremely low pretest scores (cf. Taylor 1985).

Mortality

The validity of pre- and posttest comparisons of two or more groups of students is reduced if different types or numbers of students tend to drop out of one group more (or less) than the other(s). Mortality is similar to the problem of selective attrition from the sample or cohort under investigation, discussed earlier.

External validity

Even when threats to internal validity are relatively low, the external validity, or the ability to generalize findings across subpopulations or from a sample to a population, may be questionable. Can we expect that the gains shown by freshmen entering the institution in 1985 apply to freshmen entering the institution in 1990? One's confidence in such generalizations would be especially weak for institutions undergoing change in their marketing or admissions. External validity will be a particular concern when assessment is voluntary rather than required, as students who voluntarily participate in a testing program would be expected to differ on several dimensions from students who choose not to participate.

Multiple measures

Threats to internal and external validity may be minimized but never eliminated. When outcomes assessments are potentially threatening to faculty, students, or staff, these ever-present threats to validity can become political "ammunition" to discredit or disregard information about outcomes.

One method that has been promoted for increasing assessment validity is to employ multiple measures that "converge" on the outcomes of interest (cf. Cook and Campbell 1979; Palola 1981). This approach may be useful for conceptual purposes, when available instruments do not match institutional definitions of key concepts, so that multiple instruments will provide a more useful indicator of students' development than any single instrument. Empirically, multiple measures provide an opportunity to determine the stability of key outcomes when assessed with different instruments. And multiple measures provide political advantages by providing a "weight of evidence" that reduces skepticism. A combination of standardized and locally developed instruments may also serve to satisfy external demands for accountability while simultaneously involving faculty, staff, and students in self-reflection and institutional improvement. Multiple measures do *not* offer a substitute for careful research design and test administration to avoid many of these confounds, however. In the face of confounding factors such as history, maturation, and mortality, multiple measures will only increase the magnitude of error, uncertainty, and ultimately embarrassment in assessment.

Unanticipated Effects of Assessment

As demonstrated by the experiences of Alverno College, Northeast Missouri State University, and other schools that have adopted value-added approaches, assessment is an educational intervention that modifies the same process it is designed to measure objectively. As such, assessment may have unanticipated effects on students, both negative and positive. The manner in which faculty, counselors, and administrators administer and interpret assessment programs to students will influence the reactive effects of testing, which might include:

1. *Test anxiety and stress.* This particular risk accompanies the phenomenon of bottoming out. Sensitivity to this issue in test administration, debriefing, and presentation of findings will substantially reduce this problem.
2. *Fatigue.* After spending several hours completing pre- or posttesting, students' ability to concentrate on other work may be limited. Therefore, testing should be scheduled for the times when it is least likely to interfere with ongoing class work and studying.
3. *Emphasis on test scores rather than on the process of learning.* A vigorous assessment program may suggest to students that test scores are more important than the

process of learning. "We now distribute grades and scores as if students were in a contest with each other" (Edgarton 1987, p. 109). It is the responsibility of the institution to communicate its underlying values to students and to explain why and how the test scores are useful.

4. *Better test-taking skills*. For better or for worse, assessment and evaluation are very much a part of our culture. Continued exposure to assessment in a supportive environment may help students to develop skills to cope effectively with tests and evaluations.
5. *A sense of development and growth.* Because of the relative nature of most grading, students rarely have an opportunity to document or observe their own intellectual development. Pre- and posttesting may provide students with feedback about their development. Even when individual scores are not released (and the cohort is the unit of measurement), students' experience of the instrument during posttesting relative to pretesting as well as the increase in achievement demonstrated by the group can be valuable information.
6. *Curiosity and motivation*. Although bottoming out can be stressful for students, encountering material with which one is unfamiliar can also be stimulating. Challenging and engaging assessment instruments may motivate students to acquire specialized knowledge and skills or, conversely, to broaden their knowledge and skills. When students have the opportunity to discuss their testing experience with an academic counselor or advisor, they can plan a program that responds to their experienced needs and interests.

COGNITIVE OUTCOME INSTRUMENTS

This section briefly describes more than 25 cognitive assessment instruments that can be used within a talent development perspective.

This survey of standardized, commercially available tests of cognitive abilities should not imply that such instruments are always the best solution to the challenges of measuring student outcomes or development. In fact, a number of researchers and practitioners have recently encouraged colleges and universities to develop assessment programs that go beyond testing (cf. Boyer 1987; Edgarton 1987; Mingle 1986). For example, "the important fact to note is that where an assessment program is making a difference, testing is not the sole source of information" (Banta and Fisher 1987, p. 45). In addition, locally developed devices as well as standardized instruments may in many instances prove highly useful for assessing outcomes. Two institutions that have successfully used locally designed instruments are Kean College (Kean College of New Jersey Presidential Task Force 1986) and Alverno College (Alverno College Faculty 1985).

The "best" instrument is one that most closely matches the goals and values of the institution and the structure of its curriculum.

With these caveats in mind, this section is designed to acquaint readers with a broad range of standardized instruments available for assessing outcomes. The selection of an instrument for use within a particular institution, however, requires consideration of the institutional context. From this perspective, the "best" instrument is one that most closely matches the goals and values of the institution and the structure of its curriculum (cf. Ewell 1984). As this review indicates, tests that purport to measure the same skill may vary widely in content and structure as a result of the manner in which test makers define concepts like comprehension, writing, or reasoning ability. Thus, we leave to readers the task of assessing the fit between what a specific test measures and what a specific class, major, program, or school attempts to teach.

Congruent with the talent development philosophy, it is recommended that student assessments be administered within a pretest/posttest research design. Unfortunately, few cognitive assessment instruments have been used in this manner. An important direction for future research, then, is the collection of additional empirical information about the suitability of these instruments for application in talent development. Until such information is available, faculty can best assess the quality of alternative instruments for longitudinal, repeated-measures assessments, taking into account local institutional and student characteristics.

Another frequently expressed concern about pre- and posttest assessments is whether gain scores are valid indicators of students' development (cf. Fincher 1985). The potential problem of unreliable gain scores is significantly reduced when aggregate rather than individual scores are used. Most talent development assessments require group means derived from assessments of large numbers of students. Under these conditions, gain scores should provide reasonably reliable indicators of development. Ultimately, however, unreliable gain scores are a function of the unreliability of the instrument itself.

A final concern is the possible confounding effects of practice. This issue is of particular concern for tests traditionally used in admissions, selection, and certification, because test preparation materials are often widely available for such instruments. While the effects of practice and specialized preparation on performance continue to be a topic of debate, potential users of standardized instruments should consider the possibility that gain scores may be confounded by the effects of test preparation. (By asking students to indicate how they prepared for the examination and then merging this information with test scores and descriptive student data, regression analyses can be conducted to explore the effects of different methods of test preparation.)

As noted earlier, the talent development approach to assessment does not rely on the use of any particular instrument. Rather, the appropriateness of an assessment device should be considered in light of the curricular or programmatic aims being assessed. To this end, a vast array of cognitive outcome instruments are presently available that measure outcomes the authors view as critical to higher education's mission of student development. These instruments focus on such areas of student learning as basic skills, competence in specialized subjects, and general education (or comprehensive achievement).

The instruments described in this chapter are by and large nationally normed instruments developed for a college population. This section by no means provides a comprehensive set of cognitive assessment instruments. Rather, the instruments selected represent a wide range of standardized tests that are available for use with postsecondary students. Appendix A provides an overview of the instruments included in this section.

The following descriptions reflect wherever possible the first-hand experiences of the authors. In many cases, however, secondary sources have been used. Thus, this section is intended as a point of departure rather than the last stop for selecting cognitive assessment instruments. Several reference books are especially recommended for additional information about standardized assessment instruments. Sweetland and Keyser's *Tests: A Comprehensive Reference for Assessments in Psychology, Education, and Business* (1986) provides brief, easy-to-read descriptions of a large number of cognitive assessment instruments. *The ETS Test Collection Catalog,* volume 1, *Achievement Tests and Measurement Devices* (ETS 1986) also describes cognitive assessment instruments available from a variety of sources. For critical reviews as well as descriptive information, an excellent encyclopedia is the *Mental Measurements Yearbook* (Mitchell 1985). *Test Critiques* (Keyser and Sweetland 1987) is less comprehensive than the MMY but provides thoughtful reviews.

This review is organized into three broad categories: general education tests, specific skills tests, and subject matter competency tests. General education tests include instruments that provide an integrated approach to measuring an array of cognitive abilities typically associated with core curricula or general education programs. In contrast, specific skills tests focus on a single ability, such as reading, writing, mathematical reasoning, or cognitive reasoning. Subject matter competency tests measure knowledge and skills associated with specific disciplines. (A fourth category of interest to the authors but not explored here involves assessments of vocational/practice skills for specific occupations.)

Within each category, instruments are further divided according to the target population for which they were designed: lower-division students, upper-division students, or (occasionally) a full range of college students. Taking the test level of difficulty into account reduces (but does not eliminate) the problems of bottoming out and topping out.

Typically, tests designed for lower-division students are administered as pretests for selection, placement, diagnosis, or curricular development. Useful information may be obtained by readministering these instruments as posttests, generally at the end of a student's second year of college (following the completion of the general education program, core curriculum, or lower-division requirements). Such posttests provide an opportunity to measure the change in students' performance over time on either an aggregate or individual level, as appropriate. In addition, posttests may contribute to a better understanding of the impact of the lower-division curriculum, the effectiveness of decisions about placement, and the degree to which the institution is achieving its educational goals.

On the other hand, tests designed for upper-division students are often used for admission to graduate or professional schools or for certification. Additional benefits may be obtained by pretesting with these instruments at an earlier time—for example, when students enter their selected majors or begin upper-division study. Pretesting may be useful for diagnosing students' strengths and weaknesses and for indicating the skills and abilities that students must master to reach the standards established by graduate and professional programs. Pretesting also provides an opportunity to collect baseline information against which students' performance on later posttests can be assessed. The gains shown by students will be useful for comparing the educational impact of particular programs of study and/or developmental patterns shown by different subgroups of students (assuming large enough sample sizes to provide stable comparisons).

In other words, instruments designed for other purposes may potentially support a talent development approach to assessment when administered as part of a longitudinal, repeated-measures design. As discussed in more detail later, because many institutions often use standardized instruments for selection, placement, or certification, relatively minor adjustments would be needed to readminister the instruments and thereby obtain information about students' talent development.

General Education Tests

This section describes assessment instruments that measure a range of cognitive concerns and subject areas at a level appropriate for undergraduate college students.

Instruments geared toward lower-division students (or below)

The ACT Assessment Program and College Board Scholastic Aptitude Test. These two instruments may be useful for more than their traditional applications in admissions. The ACT Academic Tests provide scores in four areas: English usage, mathematics usage, social studies reading, and natural sciences reading. These scores, as well as the composite, are presented on standard scales ranging from 1 to 36. In addition to its traditional use in admissions, ACT encourages application of results in academic counseling, guidance, placement, and orientation (Aiken 1985; Kifer 1985). In support of these aims, the ACT High School Report provides raw scores and percentile rank as well as the standard scale scores (Kifer 1985). Beyond these applications, the Academic Tests are useful for talent development purposes on a pre- and posttest basis to assess the comprehensive learning of students during the first two years of college.

The Scholastic Aptitude Test (SAT) also provides up to four scores. In addition to the verbal and mathematical scores, verbal subscores for reading and vocabulary are available, as well as results for the Test of Standard Written English. Although the SAT emphasizes mathematical skills somewhat more than the ACT (cf. Aiken 1985), evidence suggests that the ACT and SAT provide very similar information. The mathematics scales of the two tests are highly correlated, and it is possible to obtain an excellent estimate of the SAT verbal score from a combination of the English, social studies, and natural sciences scales (Astin, Henson, and Christian 1978). The use of the ACT Academic Tests and the SAT on a pre- and post-test basis represents a notable expansion of the value of these instruments beyond their traditional conception as tests of admission.

General Examinations of the College-Level Examination Program. The General Examinations of the College-Level Examination Program (CLEP) include material that is usually covered in the first two years of college. The General Examinations address five broad areas—English composition, humanities, mathematics, natural sciences, and social sciences and history—emphasizing "concepts, principles, relationships, and applications of course materials" (Sweetland and Keyser 1986, p. 374). CLEP is designed for both traditional and nontraditional students to earn college credit for skills and knowledge they may have acquired outside an academic setting.

Reviewers differ in their evaluations of the General Examinations. Some are generally positive, noting that the CLEP General Examinations "represent a reasonable balance between factual recall and application" (Dressel 1978, p. 634). Others are less sanguine, arguing that the exams do not adequately measure critical thinking and interpretation and instead emphasize factual recall and simple problem solving (Wallace 1978). And although Dressel praises the technical quality of the exams, Wallace warns that "students just completing the courses for which the CLEP tests are designed to measure equivalence generally answer fewer than half the items correctly. This could be deleterious to the score characteristics of the tests . . ." (p. 639).

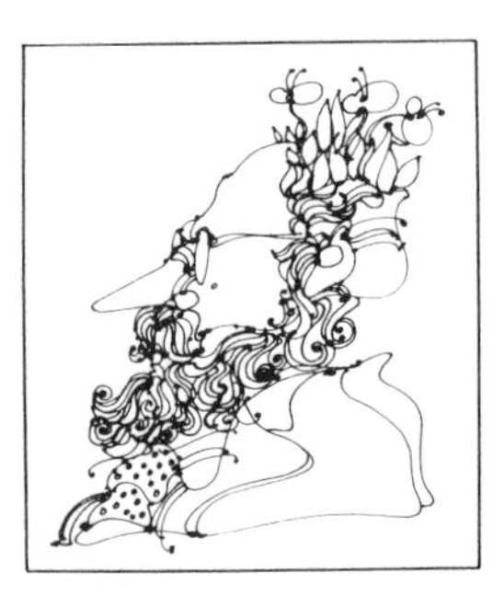

Sequential Tests of Educational Progress, series III. The Sequential Tests of Educational Progress (STEP) are similar to the CLEP in that both are designed to assess academic mastery and to assist in diagnosis. The most recent set (series III) includes seven self-contained tests designed for grade levels 10 to 12.9. (Series II, which is still available, includes some instruments for students in grades 13 and 14.) The tests measure various components of achievement in general education, including English expression, reading, mathematics, science, and social studies. The examinations are designed to emphasize application of knowledge over recall of facts.

Some concern has been expressed about both the validity and reliability of the STEP (Floden 1985), specifically about content validity of the separate instruments. Floden suggests they may be better viewed as measures of "general ability" rather than of specific skills and abilities. Another researcher recommends against the use of STEP for individual diagnosis and placement until future research establishes its validity for such purposes (Shanahan 1985).

Stanford Test of Academic Skills (1982 edition). The Stanford Test of Academic Skills (TASK) provides a comprehensive assessment of basic skills considered necessary to undertake college-level work, including reading comprehension, vocabulary, English, mathematics, science, social science, and use of information. The instrument was developed to reflect the instructional objectives of secondary schools, based on a review of textbooks, curricula, and state guides (Ory 1985). The authors' interest is in the version of TASK designed for grades 9 to 13, although another version for grades 8 to 12 is available as well. An optional writing assessment program accompanies the TASK; it is designed to measure syntax, organization, vocabulary, the quality of ideas, and general merit.

The usefulness of this instrument for talent development assessment is enhanced by the provision of raw (absolute) scores for subscales as well as for "content clusters" within subscales. Nonetheless, "one would not be interested in using

TASK if the instructional objectives used in its construction did not match the objectives of the user's school" (Ory 1985, p. 1469).

Instruments geared toward upper-division students

Graduate Record Exam. The General Test of the GRE, widely used as an admissions tool for graduate programs, offers opportunities for talent development assessments similar to those provided by the SAT. The GRE provides scores for verbal, quantitative, and analytical reasoning abilities. Use of this measure for pre- and posttesting would be most appropriate with upper-division high achievers to avoid the negative effects of bottoming out. Future analyses that offer methods for comparing performance on the SAT and GRE would significantly extend the potential applications of these measures. Further, the relativistic nature of both GRE and SAT scores reduces the usefulness of the instruments for talent development applications.

ETS Academic Profile. The Academic Profile is an innovative new instrument, now in its pilot year. It was designed for students who have completed their general education programs "to measure academic skills (college-level reading, college-level writing, critical thinking, and using mathematical data) in the context of three major discipline groups (humanities, social sciences, and natural sciences)" (Educational Testing Service 1987, p. 1). Two versions of the Academic Profile are available: a three-hour version, which includes 144 items and for which ETS provides both group and individual scores, and a one-hour short form, which includes 48 items and for which ETS provides only group scores. In addition, ETS offers an optional essay that is scored by the institution, using ETS manuals.

As part of the pilot year, ETS is conducting validation studies and actively soliciting feedback from participating institutions about the usefulness of the instrument. Because it is specifically designed for outcomes assessments and apparently avoids some of the logistical problems posed by the McBer Behavioral Event Interview and the ACT COMP Comprehensive Exam, the Academic Profile may come to fill a needed gap in the assessment of general education.

Graduate Management Admissions Test. The GMAT is the first of several instruments reviewed here that were developed as admission tests for professional school. Traditionally associated with admissions, these instruments could be used in longitudinal designs to assess the effectiveness of academic programs in preparing students for admission to professional schools. Pretesting at the beginning junior level (following completion of lower-division requirements) could be implemented by using older versions of these tests, which are published in the many preparation manuals now available commercially.

The GMAT is designed to predict success in the first year of graduate study in business. In effect, it is a "multiple-choice paper-pencil test measuring general verbal and quantitative abilities. It does not measure proficiency in undergraduate business or economics courses" (Sweetland and Keyser 1986, p. 399). Use of the GMAT on a pre- and posttest basis may be helpful for those institutions especially concerned with the educational preparation of students for admission to MBA study. Moreover, apart from the issues of construct and predictive validity that have been raised generally with the GMAT as an admissions instrument (Crosby 1985), the Practical Business Judgment section and the items that require students to interpret charts, graphs, and tables have useful face validity for talent development.

Medical College Admission Test. Relative to the GMAT, the MCAT has more utility for general education pre- and posttests, as it assesses knowledge of science (emphasizing biology, chemistry, and physics), application of science knowledge through problems in science, and varied analytical skills in reading and quantitative areas. Given the prerequisite undergraduate coursework expected in biology, physics, and general and organic chemistry, this test lends itself well to pre- and posttests.

Law School Admission Test. The LSAT may also be appropriate for talent development assessments during the undergraduate years. The post-1982 versions of this instrument include four subtests (reading comprehension, analytic reasoning, logical reasoning, and "issues and facts"). Each subtest appears to measure verbal reasoning skills, however (Melton 1985).

For purposes of talent development, a major drawback is that the Law School Admission Council reports only the total score. Consequently, student gains and losses on individual subtests of the LSAT would not normally be available. A talent development approach might be better served by the Graduate Record Examination General Test, with its separate reporting of the student's verbal, quantitative, and analytical scores. Use of the LSAT on a pre- and posttest basis appears to make most sense for those institutions interested in students' preparation for law school.

NTE Core Battery. The NTE Core Battery (formerly known as the Common Examinations of the National Teacher Examination Program) measures the academic proficiency of undergraduate students and recent graduates of teacher preparation programs (Scannell 1985b). The Core includes separate two-hour tests in communication skills, general knowledge, and professional knowledge.

The communication skills test includes subtests for listening, reading, and writing. The listening section presents material and questions via a recording and requires the examinee "to identify the content of a message or a paraphrase of the content, to identify a main idea, to evaluate, and to infer from oral signals" (Scannell 1985b, p. 1067). The reading section addresses similar analytic concerns, using passages topically related to education. The writing assessment includes multiple choice items about grammar, punctuation, and effectiveness of expression as well as an essay component, in which students are asked to relate a personal experience. Generally, only a total scale for communication skills is reported.

The test of general knowledge addresses literature and the fine arts, mathematics, and a variety of science and social science areas. While the social studies and literature and fine arts sections require students to demonstrate skills in interpretation and application of knowledge, items in the mathematics and science areas unfortunately appear to be geared more to the secondary than the postsecondary level of difficulty (Scannell 1985b). Again, only the total score for general knowledge is provided.

The test of professional knowledge addresses pedagogical issues related to teaching practices, theory, and evaluation. For an institution engaged in teacher preparation, assessment with this subtest appears to provide a comprehensive measure of the professional knowledge generally included in teacher education programs.

Based on the high intercorrelations among the three tests of the Core Battery, these scales may "measure similar knowledge and skills and . . . may not reflect distinct domains of proficiency" (Nelsen 1985, p. 1066). Nonetheless, the NTE tests may well be preferable to the alternatives for assessing the academic skills and abilities of beginning teachers (Nelsen 1985). Although generally administered to college seniors who are preparing to enter the teaching profession, the NTE Core Battery seems well suited for earlier pretest administration as part of a longitudinal research design. In fact, NTE encourages the use of the Core Battery for both "standardized examination of academic achievement for college students entering or in teacher education programs *and* for college seniors completing such programs" (quoted in Quellmalz 1985, p. 1188).

NTE Pre-Professional Skills Test. Basic proficiencies needed for a teaching career are also the focus of the Pre-Professional Skills Tests (PPSTs) of the National Teacher Examination Program. The PPST includes separate instruments for reading, mathematics, and writing. Both the reading and mathematics tests are multiple choice, while the writing test includes both multiple choice and an essay.

The PPST is administered both to students interested in entering teacher training programs (as an admissions tool) and also to students who are completing such programs (as part of the certification process) (Bauernfeind 1987). While these applications (as well as the ability to derive raw scores from the scaled scores provided) suggest that the PPST may be appropriate for talent development assessments, readers should be aware of several concerns reviewers have expressed.

The PPST, for example, has been criticized for its emphasis on minimum standards; institutions might consider forgoing tests of "minimum competency" in favor of alternative instruments that focus on "college-level mastery" (Quellmalz 1985). Further, the NTE is unclear about the target audience(s) for the test, and high correlations between the reading and math subtests suggest that one or both of these tests may confound measurement of the basic skills (Quellmalz 1985). And the content validity of the PPST essentially reflects subjective judgments about the knowledge that is important for future teachers (or others) to master (Bauernfeind 1987).

Instruments geared toward all levels of college students

ACT College Outcomes Measures Project. The ACT COMP represents an innovative approach to measuring outcomes. This test battery was designed to measure "general" outcomes of college or students' abilities "to apply specific facts and concepts in work, family, and community roles" (Forrest and Steele 1982, p. 1). That is, the tests attempt to go beyond specific course content to measure the more general abilities and competencies that are often identified as the goals of general and liberal education. The COMP is designed to measure students' competence in three content areas (functioning within social institutions, using science and technology, and using the arts) and three process areas (communicating, solving problems, and clarifying values). ACT offers two forms of the COMP, a six-hour composite form and a shorter (under three hours) objective form.

In both forms, students are required to respond to a variety of stimuli, including text, audio tapes, and films. In the composite form, response modes also vary, including multiple choice, short answers, essays, and tape-recorded speeches. The objective form includes only multiple-choice responses. ACT has conducted (and will disseminate upon request) several studies to establish the validity and reliability of the instruments for different populations.

COMP scores are provided in a detailed profile, with scores for each subtest presented as a percentile relative to the normative group. This relative scaling system somewhat limits the test's usefulness for talent development assessment.

ACT has attempted to fill an important gap in the range of assessment options with the COMP, but several characteristics of the composite test limit its usefulness. First, administration of the composite form of the COMP is time consuming and complex, requiring numerous audiovisual devices, two separate sittings, and six hours of testing time. Students' fatigue, equipment failures, and other logistical problems can severely reduce the validity of COMP scores. The talent development approach compounds these problems, as both pre- and posttesting is needed. After once experiencing the difficulty and length of the pretest, students may be reluctant to participate in a posttest

(Astin and Ayala 1987). ACT recognizes the importance of student recruitment and offers some assistance in this area.

The objective form is shorter and simpler and is the form that higher education institutions have used most often. While logistical problems and costs are reduced, the benefits of multiple options for response are lost. Further, the objective form yields scores that are accurate at the aggregate level only, whereas the comprehensive form yields scores that may be appropriately used for measurement for individuals.

McBer Behavioral Event Interview. The Behavioral Event Interview (BEI), an integral part of the Student Potential Program of the Council for Adult and Experiential Learning (CAEL), is designed to identify a broad range of students' talents and potential that relate to success in education. The BEI involves a one-hour, in-depth probing strategy that elicits information of a critical incident nature. The trained interviewer evaluates the data, coding the behavioral insights from the interview as evidence of specific capabilities, which range from initiative, persistence, and planning skill to self-confidence, influence, and leadership talents.

An evaluation of this assessment procedure suggests that "the BEI has a significant degree of construct validity" (Astin, Inouye, and Korn 1986, p. 32). The instrument can effectively be applied to predict student outcomes, including grades and academic progress. Despite these positive indicators, further evaluation of the BEI is recommended with larger sample sizes than have previously been obtained. Further, the BEI should be used in longitudinal assessments to explore the institutional and educational factors that facilitate growth on this measure (Astin, Inouye, and Korn 1985). Administration of the BEI, however, requires that an institution provide time and money to obtain the special training for interviewers needed for this time-consuming process.

Specific Skills Tests

Tests reviewed in this section focus on a single skill, often considered of critical importance in undergraduate education, including writing, reading, mathematical reasoning, verbal reasoning, and critical thinking.

Instruments geared toward lower-division students

College Board English Composition Test with essay. This test has two parts: an essay question and a set of 60 multiple-choice items pertaining to such concerns as idiomatic expression, usage, grammar, and diction. Instructions for the relatively brief (20-minute) essay direct examinees "to plan and write an essay, agreeing or disagreeing with a statement provided and supporting their opinion with specific examples from personal experience or knowledge" (Scannell 1985a, pp. 357–58). The exam is scored by the testing agency, with each essay read independently by two trained readers. This scoring service is not inexpensive, however, which explains the test's present schedule of administration—once a year (usually in December) at test centers established by the College Board.

Two components of the CLEP General Examination, reviewed in the previous section, offer alternative approaches to the assessment of writing skills. The CLEP General Examination in English Composition, edition two, measures college-level competency in a similar two-part approach, with an essay section and a 65-question objective section, the latter dealing primarily with logic and sentence structure (Sweetland and Keyser 1986). Whereas the College Board English Composition test allocates only 20 minutes for the essay, this test has a 45-minute essay in which students are asked to present logical arguments and evidence to support a particular point of view.

In addition, the CLEP Humanities (Freshman English) test offers an optional essay section to accompany a set of objective questions (Sweetland and Keyser 1986). The Freshman English test allocates 90 minutes for the optional essay, significantly longer than the CLEP and the College Board composition tests. During this time, the student is called upon to deal with three writing tasks in which "the topics present concrete problems involving personal knowledge and require control and flexibility in the use of language" (p. 382).

Potential users of any of these three composition tests should recognize that they are instruments assessing "standard" or "textbook" English competency on the part of entering or first-year college students, an especially important consideration for those institutions with populations whose English skills are not standard. Further, a low level of reliability is a frequent problem with any essay test (Bauernfeind 1987). A third consideration involves resources—personnel and financial. The 90-minute optional essay section of the Freshman English subject examination is designed to be graded by personnel from the examinee's institution, calling for the commitment of significant staff and faculty time. Where the essay is a required part of the

Potential users of any of these three composition tests should recognize that they are instruments assessing "standard" or "textbook" English competency.

instrument, however (as in both the CLEP and College Board examinations), the testing organization provides a grading service.

Nelson-Denny Reading Test, forms E and F. The Nelson-Denny Reading Test focuses on the development of skills in three major areas of reading ability: vocabulary development, reading comprehension, and reading rate. Each form of the test includes two subtests, vocabulary and comprehension, both using a multiple-choice format. With the 100 items in the vocabulary subtest, students are to choose from five options the one that best completes a sentence or defines a word. Similarly, on the comprehension subtest, the examinee responds to 36 multiple-choice questions related to eight passages covering such areas as the humanities, science, and social science. It is also from reading the first of these passages that an individual's rate is determined—the number of words read by one minute into the passage.

Although the Nelson-Denny is widely used, reviewers raise several important questions about its usefulness for college students. While the instrument is normed for secondary and college students, "the test does not discriminate well among good readers" (Hambleton 1987, p. 476). The Nelson-Denny sample underrepresents blacks and Latinos and students from regions with significant enrollment in "major" institutions (Ysseldyke 1985). Further, the reading passages sampled "do not appear representative of the text types students will regularly confront in science, mathematics, vocational education, and other courses" (Tierney 1985, p. 1036), and it is questionable whether the test has "precision and generalizability" to support its use for diagnostic and placement decisions (Tierney 1985). To ameliorate these problems, institutions should review the fit between test content and curriculum content before using the test (Van Meter and Herrmann 1986–87).

Writing Proficiency Program. Its publisher describes the Writing Proficiency Program as a "criterion-referenced assessment and instructional system." The assessment instruments are only one component of a comprehensive writing program geared toward students in grades 11 through 13. Because the program includes both an initial test (pretest) and a mastery test (posttest), the assessment component may be useful for talent development applications. Each instrument includes both multiple-choice and essay questions. The course instructor scores the exams, which yield subscores for a variety of technical and expressive aspects of writing. Given the absence of empirical information about test reliability and validity, however, this package is likely to be most useful as a resource for institutions interested in developing their own writing assessments (cf. Polloway 1985).

Instruments geared toward upper-division students

Western Michigan English Qualifying Examination. The Western Michigan English Qualifying Exam (EQE) is used to gauge students' levels of English usage skills. This 195-item assessment tool addresses "grammatical errors (30 items), punctuation for meaning (45 items), sentence structure (30 items), spelling (30 items), word usage (30 items), and reading comprehension and rhetorical style (30 items)" (Sweetland and Keyser 1986, p. 247). Designed for measuring the English skills of college juniors through entering graduate students, the EQE uses items taken from the written work of students at this level.

The EQE seems appropriate for use on a longitudinal basis with upper-division students. Pretesting with this instrument during the junior year is potentially useful for diagnostic purposes, while subsequent retesting during the senior year would provide a posttest measure of change.

Doppelt Mathematical Reasoning Test. Developed as "a high-level measure of mathematical skills comparable to the Miller Analogies Test" (Sweetland and Keyser 1983, p. 254), the Doppelt is widely used as a measure of mathematical reasoning ability in the selection of students for graduate work. Given this design, administering the instrument as a pretest to juniors followed by exit-year posttesting would be one potentially useful application of the talent development approach.

Pre- and posttesting with this instrument could provide colleges and universities a measure of their curricular impact and of individual student's growth in this skill area. Institutions with interest in this 50-problem multiple-choice test should be aware, however, that "apparently no systematic approach has been made to determine how valuable the test is for graduate students in other areas" besides mathematics and statistics (Clemens 1965, p. 725).

Furthermore, potential talent development users of the Doppelt should note that "none of the problems involve mathematics beyond the usual secondary school level" (Clemens 1965, p. 725), an observation that reflects generally on the mathematical literacy of college students. How this fact matches institutional expectations for students' basic skill development in this domain is thus an essential consideration for users. Further research seems called for to determine the utility of this instrument for talent development assessment with different college populations.

Miller Analogies Test. The Miller Analogies Test (MAT) is well known as an instrument designed to aid admission to graduate school by measuring verbal reasoning skills. The test includes 100 items, each of which requires the student to select, from multiple options, the best completion to an analogy. The authors' major concern is not with issues of predictive validity that preoccupy so many others. Rather, the talent development approach leads to an interest in better defining the cognitive skills measured by the instrument. In this regard, the MAT is a difficult test that "measures largely verbal comprehension in the context of general information" (Willingham 1965, p. 749).

For institutions wishing to assess such verbal ability, this instrument has multiple pre- and posttest benefits. The MAT provides information about verbal skills and is widely accepted as a tool for graduate admissions. Consequently, institutions using the MAT might obtain longitudinal data that could be periodically compared with standards set for entering graduate students in a variety of disciplines. A special strength of the MAT is its "high ceiling," or its ability to differentiate among students with high levels of verbal ability (Geisinger 1987). Further, the MAT yields absolute (not relativistic) scores, and item analyses can be obtained by administering widely available "practice tests." A potential weakness of the MAT, however, is that individual scores can be significantly improved through test training (Geisinger 1987). When used in longitudinal assessments, such training effects may confound the measurement of actual increases in verbal abilities.

Instruments geared toward all levels of college students

Watson-Glaser Critical Thinking Appraisal, forms A and B. The Watson-Glaser Critical Thinking Appraisal is designed to measure adults' ability in an area that is frequently identified as an important goal of higher education (Woehlke 1987). This ability is increasingly important as both an educational goal and a focus of evaluation in selecting employees (Helmstadter 1985). The Watson-Glaser includes five subtests: inference, recognition of assumptions, deduction, interpretation, and evaluation of arguments.

In this 40-minute test, examinees contend with 80 items (16 per subtest) that require them to recognize both valid arguments and inconsistencies in reasoning and to demonstrate their level of skill in making inferences and noting implications from statements. The Watson-Glaser is geared to a ninth grade reading level, even though it clearly calls for reasoning skills that are above that level, but in this way it largely avoids contaminating the assessment of critical thinking abilities with reading abilities. In content, the items include both neutral and more controversial topics, focusing on problems and issues of data interpretation likely to be encountered through contemporary media.

Although reviewers generally regard the Watson-Glaser as a well-constructed test, some cautions are necessary (Berger 1985). First, the test does not clearly distinguish between items designed to be neutral versus those designed to be more controversial. Second, this instrument assesses critical thinking only through reading; one can but speculate as to the comparability of findings were students' critical thinking abilities assessed with a listening test.

Yet another caution relates to using Watson-Glaser assessment data for advising individual students. The subtest scores are based on a small number of items, which the authors recognize as constituting insufficient reliability for individual evaluation or diagnosis. But for talent development purposes, these subtest scores have utility for the analysis of the critical thinking abilities at an aggregate level, which in turn could be related to the types of critical thinking training that might be most needed by such groups.

Finally, the utility of the test largely depends on one's level of agreement with the operational definition of critical thinking embodied by the Watson-Glaser (Berger 1985; Helmstadter 1985).

Cornell Critical Thinking Test, level Z. Those with interest in the assessment of critical thinking have an alternative instrument available with the Cornell Critical Thinking Test, level Z, designed for grades 13 and over. Like the Watson-Glaser, the Cornell Test is designed to assess talents for critical thinking of college students and other older adults. Through 52 items, divided into seven sections, this test seeks to assess such abilities as detecting equivocal argument, evaluating the reliability of observations, judging the authenticity of sources, and discovering various types of assumptions.

The American Psychological Association has rated the technical construction of Watson-Glaser above the Cornell test (Woehlke 1987). The adequacy of either test for a talent development approach, however, should be judged by the particulars of an institution's curriculum in this area. The correct choice requires close examination of the fit between the goals of the curriculum and the skills measured by the assessment instruments.

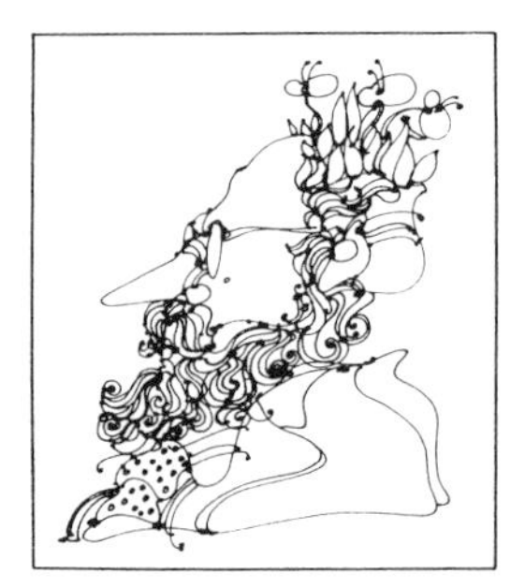

Goyer Organization of Ideas Test, form S. The Goyer Organization of Ideas Test (GOIT) is a 30-minute, multiple-choice test focusing on various aspects of one's ability to organize ideas verbally. GOIT test takers are faced with questions about outlining, with items on the ordering of statements, and with items that require selection of the most appropriate word, phrase, premise, or unifying statement.

"Although the test measures something consistently, it is unclear if that something is a generalized organizational skill or the content of an introductory speech communication class" (Brown 1985, p. 618). The GOIT may be particularly useful, however, "for measuring the effect of efforts to upgrade the skills embodied in its terms" (Frary 1985, p. 619). What we might have, then, is a relevant assessment instrument for courses where organizational skills are taught.

The GOIT requires a relatively high level of reading ability (Frary 1985), and the test may confound the organizational constructs it is designed to measure with "general verbal ability" (p. 619). A final concern is that the normative data provided are inadequate, drawn from a sample that is not representative of either a college student or general adult population.

Subject Matter Competency Tests

This section considers some of the instruments available to assess students' mastery of diverse subject matter. The extensive range of curricular specialties prohibits a comprehensive review, and the presentation consequently emphasizes examination programs with a variety of subject matter tests. The institutional utility of these tests in a talent development approach, however, depends on their relevance to the actual curriculum content taught. Faculty must review each assessment instrument to determine how well it addresses the various subject matter competencies expected of students by their particular disciplines.

Instruments geared toward lower-division students

Advanced Placement Program of the College Entrance Examination Board. This Educational Testing Service–College Board production is "designed to assess achievement, place entering college students, and assist in granting credit to students who have done college-level work in secondary school" (ETS 1980, p. 12). Although designed for administration in high schools, those students who elect to take these exams demonstrate relatively high levels of cognitive skill and preparation for postsecondary education.

The Advanced Placement Program represents a major effort, with examinations that relate to 24 introductory college courses in 13 fields: biology, chemistry, physics, French, German, Latin, Spanish, mathematics, music, computer science, English, history, and art. With no test longer than three hours, these paper-and-pencil instruments (of a largely multiple-choice, objective nature) have potential to efficiently gauge students' learning, especially for lower-division students.

Unfortunately, the grading procedures employed by ETS significantly constrain the use of the Advanced Placement Program for talent development aims. With examinations graded on a five-point scale, an institution obtains only a crude estimate of students' learning. Information that relates to specific items or subfields of knowledge and to the particular cognitive or curricular objectives of a college academic program is not provided. Another barrier to the use of the Advanced Placement exams for talent development purposes is their cost: ETS currently charges $53 per person per test. Under these conditions, the contributions of the program are probably limited simply to serving as a placement tool for the institution and as a way to earn credit for the degree seeker.

College Board Achievement Tests. The Educational Testing Service also offers a variety of subject matter tests comparable to those of the Advanced Placement Program. The primary use of these Achievement Tests, however, seems more for admissions and for the prediction of students' performance in college courses. Still, as they are designed for use with students in grades 11 through 13, colleges and universities could readminister these 60-minute, paper-and-pencil tests as measures of talent development.

Instruments geared toward upper-division students
GRE subject tests. Usually viewed as a graduate admissions assessment program, the GRE test results of graduating seniors in these subject matter exams might have additional usefulness for talent development. Earlier pretest administration of the GRE would provide an institution with baseline data against which to assess cognitive outcomes on exit; however, the full benefit of this pre- and posttest approach is again limited to the aggregate level, given the GRE's scaled scores. Despite the absence of sufficient subtest or item information, the talent development use of the GRE should enable academic departments and programs to more adequately assess both their effect on the learning of student cohorts and the appropriateness of their curricular preparation, as measured by this nationally normed instrument.

NTE Specialty Area Tests. The NTE Specialty Area Tests provide opportunities to assess competency in 26 fields of study, including such teaching-related areas as art and music education, early childhood education, and the teaching of reading, social studies, and speech communication. The Specialty Area Tests are intended to measure the knowledge and abilities of students who have majored in the area(s) assessed by the tests (Scannell 1985b). If students were pretested with the relevant instrument upon selection of a major and then posttested upon formal completion of requirements in the major, a helpful talent development assessment would be available in that selected subject. Thus, the concern is not with issues of predictive validity that seem to surround these instruments but with what the data add to our understanding of students' achievement and instructional impact.

Instruments geared toward all levels of college students
ACT Proficiency Examination Program. The College Proficiency Exams address a wide range of competence in subject

matter. Developed as part of the New York State Regents External Degree Program, the ACT Proficiency Examination Program (PEP) offers 49 tests: 31 objective, seven essay, and 11 that combine objective and essay components. Eighteen of the examinations are in the accounting, marketing, finance, and diverse management areas; still others have relevance to such professional fields as nursing, education, and criminal justice; and others are concerned with history (American or Afro-American), Shakespeare, earth science, physical geology, or anatomy and physiology (Mitchell 1985).

Primarily aimed at assessing proficiency in subject matter attained outside the usual classroom setting, this ACT program provides a basis for awarding college credit and placing returning students in appropriate classes. The instruments in the program seem especially appropriate to the talent development needs of institutions with nontraditional students who bring significant postsecondary learning experiences to their college career. These tests should be reviewed, however, to establish their utility for institutions with more traditional college populations. Pretest and posttest administration of these tests may be especially useful for considering the contribution of various academic programs to the types of knowledge desired by increasingly career-minded undergraduates.

CLEP Subject Examinations. Like the ACT Proficiency Examination Program, CLEP Subject Examinations serve as a vehicle for awarding college credit for knowledge acquired outside the usual classroom. This broad effort by ETS provides 46 subject matter tests in such categories as business, composition and literature, foreign languages, history and social sciences, and the sciences and mathematics. Given the range of influences (formal and informal) to which a learner is exposed, these CLEP-type examinations appear to offer instruments suited to assessment of competence in subject matter of a student body with quite diverse learning experiences.

As with other ETS–College Board instruments, full talent development benefits are limited by the lack of specific information on responses. When an optional essay section of a subject exam is administered, however, the institution has the responsibility of grading the essay, which for talent development advocates presents an opportunity to assess students' learning on a pre- and posttest basis. While this requirement means a significant commitment of staff and faculty input and time, institutions are able to assess what is important to them, with their own criteria.

Cooperative Examination Program of the American Chemical Society. The Examinations Committee of the American Chemical Society (ACS) has over the years developed an extensive effort to assess the various aspects of chemistry. Whether the concern is with general chemistry, biochemistry, organic-inorganic, electroanalytical, or physical chemistry, ACS has an instrument designed to measure the student's level of competency (Mitchell 1985).

Some are designed for use with a terminal, one-semester course, such as the Brief Physical Chemistry examination. Other ACS instruments, such as the Organic Chemistry examination, are geared to a full-year curriculum. In turn, the instruments range in administration time from 75 minutes (for the General-Organic-Biological examination, designed for those in an allied health sciences program) to 115 minutes (suggested for the ACS Examination in Organic Chemistry).

One ACS offering that should be of special interest is the Toledo Chemistry Placement Examination, designed to assess the chemistry background of entering freshmen and then determine the level at which they should continue their study. This ACS instrument most readily manifests talent development value for the institutional user. On a pretest, the results provide a measure of individual and aggregate achievement useful to decisions about academic placement. When readministered as a posttest, the data can indicate both students' progress and instructional impact in this subject.

Similarly, pre- and posttest use of other ACS instruments shows students' change in competence in subject matter. For those who view retesting with the same instrument as a demonstration of test mastery rather than change in competency, however, consideration should be given to using both a current and older form of the test in question. Keep in mind, however, that the ACS examination program periodically updates its exams and removes older forms from circulation.

Single-subject competency tests. The Duke University Political Science Information Test (American Government), the Harvard-MLA Tests of Chinese Language Proficiency, the Sare-Sanders American Government and Constitution Tests, the Cass-Sanders Psychology Test, and the Test of Spanish and

Latin American Life and Culture all represent an effort to assess a single subject, providing institutions with measures for these special interests. Some may have been developed in response to the assessment needs associated with a particular course, as is the case of the Cass-Sanders test for a first course in psychology. Others seem to have been the outcome of a special institutional effort (for example, the Duke University or Harvard-MLA venture). With just such assessment initiatives, administered before and after, an institution of higher education places itself in a position to gauge more directly its impact on students' learning over time. Beyond their specific cognitive emphasis, however, these instruments point to the possibility of institutions' devising their own measures for assessment. They demonstrate that schools can design their own instruments for areas of special concern to them, especially when adequate assessment instruments are lacking. Specifically designed assessment that is geared to a college's or university's actual curricular efforts is indeed integral to the talent development approach described in this work.

INCREASING THE USEFULNESS OF OUTCOMES ASSESSMENTS

A successful student outcomes project not only measures impact: It also *produces* impact. The successful project becomes a tool for administrators, trustees, faculty, students, and external reviewers to use in evaluation and decision making. Yet all too often, outcomes assessments fall short of this goal (Astin 1977; Baird 1976; Bowen 1980; Ewell 1983; Weiss 1988).

A successful student outcomes project not only measures impact: It also* produces *impact.

The difficulties of applying research findings to curriculum, policy, and program development are not unique to higher education. Utilization studies have repeatedly indicated that practitioners from a variety of disciplines and settings often neglect relevant research and evaluation data (Ciarlo 1981; Knorr 1977). In response to such observations, evaluation researchers have increasingly turned their attention to the use of assessment data in program and policy development (Weiss 1988). This section reviews some literature on use and discusses its application to student outcomes assessment.

Several aspects of the talent development perspective contribute to bridging the gap between researchers and practitioners. By rejecting an adversarial approach to evaluation in favor of an informational approach, the talent development perspective reduces defensiveness and hostility to evaluation. By emphasizing longitudinal designs with pre- and posttesting, talent development assessments reduce the ambiguity of assessment findings; researchers and practitioners are more likely to agree on the interpretation of the results. Evaluation data are most likely to influence decision making when top administrators and researchers agree on the goals of the institution and the goals of the assessment and perceive information about outcomes as an important source of feedback about organizational effectiveness (Weiss and Bucuvalas 1977). The talent development approach addresses each of these issues and thereby provides a framework that researchers, faculty, administrators, students, and others can share.

Before discussing more specifically the factors that promote or hinder utilization of data about outcomes, we need to define utilization. How do we know whether the research findings have been used? If we think of utilization as a continuum rather than a dichotomy, then what level of utilization might we strive for or accept as sufficient?

For the most part, researchers in applied outcomes hope that their findings may be "directly translated into political measures and action strategies" (Knorr 1977). When this situation occurs, researchers will see their recommendations widely read, discussed, and adopted.

While this approach may represent an ideal model, data are often used in other ways:

- To focus attention on an issue or to generate activity related to the issue. For example, the recent evaluative reports on higher education have served a generative function by stimulating discussion and activity about the quality of postsecondary education.
- To delay, substitute for, or legitimate a policy decision. Administrators may stall action on an issue by requesting a research project to "collect additional information" or "make sure all the facts are in." Or the administrator may use data about outcomes to support a decision that has been made for other reasons.

Information about outcomes is sometimes most useful in establishing a context for decision making rather than in establishing the single correct decision (Ewell 1983). "Increased use of student-outcomes information often leads to changes in the way certain kinds of decisions are approached—in the kinds of alternatives considered, for example—rather than changes in the substance of decisions" (p. 48). "What is needed is information that supports negotiation rather than information calculated to point out the 'correct' decision" (Cronbach and Associates 1980, p. 4).

Research findings are only one of many things that practitioners typically consider in decision making and planning (Weiss 1988; Weiss and Bucuvalas 1977). In the assessment of institutional performance, data about outcomes are supplemented by a variety of information, including subjective impressions, informal interactions, anecdotes, committee reports and recommendations, reports by external funding and accreditation agencies, and institutional ratings and reputation. Further, while researchers may be convinced of the validity of their data relative to other evidence, the administrator may see no reason to elevate research findings above other sources of information. And while researchers often assume that decision making within the institution is a rational process, it is in fact subjective and unsystematic (cf. Weick 1979).

Facilitators of Useful Research

How then can researchers encourage campus leaders to apply data about outcomes in decision making? This section discusses a variety of factors that increase the likelihood that data about outcomes will be applied to curriculum, policy, or program development.

Involvement

The literature on use of outcomes and evaluation shows consensus on the importance of involving practitioners in research, from the initial conceptualization of the research questions to the content and organization of the final report. "The greater the level of participation of potential users in the various phases of the project, the more likely users are to identify with the success of the project" (Siegel and Tucker 1985, p. 323).

Similarly, useful research emerges from an action research perspective that requires interpersonal and political as well as technical abilities (Buhl and Lindquist 1981). Action research is characterized by communication between researchers and key practitioners for the duration of a project on outcomes. In addition to research skills, the active researcher must develop facilitative skills and networking and information diffusion skills and must learn about alternative administrative and faculty practices (Lindquist 1981).

In addition, reporting should be a continuous activity, not only the final activity (Guba and Lincoln 1981). The researcher and the target audiences must interact in producing judgments and recommendations.

A review of 20 case studies from the evaluations filed at the Office of Health Evaluation of the U.S. Department of Health, Education, and Welfare concludes that use strongly depends on personal and interpersonal factors (Patton et al. 1977). If research is to have an impact, somebody must care about it and must have the leadership ability, energy, and commitment to ensure that the research receives attention. Institutional researchers can facilitate this process by identifying key decision makers and by working collaboratively with them to provide relevant and credible information.

Involvement of practitioners provides both direct and indirect benefits. Among the former are assurance that practitioners are aware of the research project, that the research addresses issues of concern to them, that the methods used are credible, and that the results are presented in a format that facilitates use. Involvement of decision makers also provides indirect benefits by increasing participants' sense of investment in, or ownership of, the project. They will be less likely to neglect a report that incorporates their suggestions and concerns, and they will be more interested in seeing the project succeed as a consequence of contributing to its development. They will be more likely to trust the researcher and to perceive him or her as competent for having taken the time to consult with campus leaders and respond appropriately to their suggestions.

A number of activities can be used to increase decision makers' involvement in research (Lindquist 1981). For example, participants can be asked to listen to taped interviews and analyze them together. Before data analysis, decision makers can be exposed to the raw data or to preliminary tabulations and asked to indicate the types of analyses they would most like to see. Brainstorming sessions can be scheduled after data analysis to generate recommendations and discuss the implications of the findings.

The participants in the collaborative process should include not only the identified "client" (that is, the administrator or department that requested the research) but also all the potential audiences for the research, which would probably include a range of administrators, program personnel, faculty, and students (Dawson and D'Amico 1985; Deshler 1984; Guba and Lincoln 1981; Moran 1987).

The involvement of practitioners in the research process is a necessary, but not sufficient, element of useful research. For example, such involvement will not be fruitful if stake holders in the assessment hold conflicting assumptions and values about the goals of the institution or of the assessment. Thus, before involving practitioners directly in the design of an outcomes assessment, the researcher may need to resolve conflicts in value.

Values

The choice of outcomes to assess, the instruments used, sampling and analysis procedures, the selection of comparison groups, and the organization of the final report are all value-based to some extent. Utilization is enhanced when both practitioners and researchers accept the same underlying model or theory of student outcomes and agree on the importance of assessing specific outcomes among particular students in a certain manner.

Research based on models or theories different from those held by decision makers is likely to be perceived as inappropriately oriented and therefore irrelevant. "It is important to stress that while [outcomes] information . . . should be as accurate as feasible, standards of accuracy are less important than are standards of relevance" (Ewell 1984, pp. 57–58).

The talent development approach provides opportunities for researchers and practitioners to clarify their implicit values and beliefs. Discussions among faculty, administrators, students, trustees, and legislators about educational and developmental priorities are a crucial element in designing assessments of outcomes. The resulting longitudinal assessment reflects institutional values by focusing on the outcomes of most importance to those involved in the assessment.

By involving practitioners in the design and analysis of research and by clarifying previously implicit values and assumptions, the researcher is attending to process issues. Process threats to utilization can be further reduced by acquiring support for the assessment from institutional leaders.

Support of top administration

The support of top administrators is often crucial to the use of research results. Chief executive officers should communicate to their managers and administrators the importance of the project to create a climate on campus that is receptive to the data (Forrest 1981). And utilization can be increased when administrators offer incentives to those willing to undertake "information-based qualitative improvements in programs and services" (Ewell 1984, p. 58). Administrative support has certain advantages:

> *Any effort at dissemination [of research data] is unlikely to be successful unless the top administration clearly supports the project. Strong administrative backing serves at least two critical functions: it provides committee members with an incentive to move ahead with the project and to find policy-relevant recommendations in the data; and it maximizes the chances that recommendations will be put into action* (Astin 1976, p. 65).

Technical factors

The issues involving process are necessary but not sufficient in conducting useful research. Reviews of utilization demonstrate that the quality of the research is also positively associated with utilization (Forrest 1981; Guba and Lincoln 1981; Kinnick 1985). An issue that many researchers have ignored, however, is the interaction of technical and political factors, such that some research is subject to extensive methodological criticism while other research, sometimes of questionable quality, wins acceptance quite easily. Especially in academic settings, technical criticisms of research may mask other motives for disregarding the data.

Interviews with 200 decision makers in mental health administration found that quality of research was an important predictor of use (Weiss and Bucuvalas 1980). Respondents rated quality of research as the single most important factor in determining their own likelihood of using research in decision making but as only the second most important factor (behind "action orientation") in determining use by others. Thus, attributional patterns and social desirability may have influenced respondents' ratings.

The actual importance of the quality of research to its use is also questionable, as members of an organization often claim to support a rational model of decision making that may have little correspondence to their actual decision-making patterns (McClintock 1984; cf. Campbell 1984).

The perfect study of outcomes has not yet been conducted and never will be, and all outcomes research is therefore subject to methodological criticism. Probably the best way to avoid politically motivated criticism of methodology is to involve potential critics in the design of the project. Under this approach, debates about research methods occur before rather than after data collection and analysis, and target audiences are less likely to dismiss results emanating from a research design they had a part in shaping.

Because the methodological challenges in outcomes research have been reviewed previously, a comprehensive review of technical factors is not provided here. The literature about utilization of social science data raises a number of additional issues for consideration, however.

First, qualitative approaches can often be a useful supplement to quantitative methods. Qualitative data provide a behind-the-scenes look at statistical data that can render research reports more interesting and less intimidating to decision makers. For example, case studies are recommended for four purposes: to chronicle, to characterize, to teach, and to test

(Guba and Lincoln 1981). This approach is often dangerous, however, because qualitative or anecdotal information may distort or misrepresent the actual meaning of quantitative findings. A case study of a "useful" program evaluation describes the use of an "interactive methodology" that combined qualitative and quantitative data to inform administrative decision making (Moran 1987).

Second, qualitative data alone are generally insufficient to satisfy the concerns of target audiences. Data about outcomes are most likely to be applied to policy development when objective techniques are used (Forrest 1981). An important element is comparative data that allow decision makers to compare findings against some meaningful norm or standard. A finding that 12 percent of graduating seniors go on to graduate or professional school, for example, has more meaning when decision makers know that the figure is 24 percent for similar schools or was 8 percent two years ago (cf. Kinnick 1985).

Third, because practitioners often have difficulty basing important decisions on a single study, survey, or test, convergent findings can lead to more confidence in the accuracy of data about outcomes. Some writers recommend that researchers adopt a strategy of multiple perspectives (Palola and Lehmann 1976). This approach has five components: multiple observers of students' learning, multiple methods of assessment, multiple standards for evaluating students' learning, multiple decision makers using data for a variety of policy issues, and multiple time periods for measuring change in students' learning. In this manner, decision makers' concerns about any one approach could be reduced by providing convergent or alternative measures. Further, the multiple perspectives approach maximizes opportunities to apply the research to various policy issues within the university. A "multimodel" for evaluation research is recommended, to include multiple perspectives, levels, methods, functions, impacts, reporting formats, and so on (Scriven 1983).

A number of researchers with experience in value-added assessment report on the benefits of multiple measures. "Together, different kinds of measures of the same outcome dimension undoubtedly provide a full picture of the dynamics of a particular educational experience" (Ewell 1983, p. 63; cf. Banta and Fisher 1987; McClain and Krueger 1985; Mentkowski and Loacker 1985).

Dissemination

The manner in which research findings are disseminated significantly influences the extent to which and the manner in which the findings are used in decision making. Ideally, dissemination is an ongoing process of communication between researchers and practitioners. It should be conceptualized as a mutual exchange between researchers and target audiences rather than as a flow of information in one direction (from researcher to decision maker) only. In this way, the final report becomes a product of the collaboration between researchers and administrators, and administrators are therefore more likely to perceive it as useful (Forrest 1981; Guba and Lincoln 1981).

Congruent with multiple perspectives, a variety of methods of dissemination can be employed, ranging from informal brainstorming sessions to formal, written reports. A number of researchers suggest that several different reports should be prepared, each one tailored to the specific concerns of target audiences (Ewell 1983; Forrest 1981).

When communication between researchers and administrators has been ongoing and open, the final report will contain no major surprises. Although many researchers believe their data may receive more attention if the findings are unexpected, counterintuitive findings are instead likely to be dismissed or ignored (cf. Guba and Lincoln 1981), which is not meant to suggest that only findings that confirm decision makers' beliefs or knowledge will gain recognition. Rather, unexpected results should be communicated to target audiences at an early stage to provide opportunities for decision makers to assimilate the new information and avoid defensive reactions.

Timing

The timing of reports is a crucial factor in use of results. One approach is to release reports when funding decisions are being made, as student outcomes may provide information about the effectiveness of existing programs, the need for additional services, or the need for program or curricular revisions (cf. Siegel and Tucker 1985). If the study is being sponsored by a campus committee or department, researchers must strive to deliver the final product on schedule. A possible exception is when other events occurring at the time would overshadow the release of the report on outcomes; under such conditions, the researcher might wait until the audience(s) would be more likely to pay attention to the findings (cf. Siegel and Tucker 1985).

Recommendations

Some disagreement emerges in the literature regarding the risks and benefits of providing recommendations for action based on research findings as opposed to simply presenting the data and allowing practitioners to develop their own recommendations. Not surprisingly, recommendations for incremental changes have met with less opposition from policy makers than recommendations for fundamental changes.

> *In some instances recommendations that state goals (ends) are more effective than those that delineate specific courses of action. This provides direction to users while permitting them considerable latitude in selecting ways of achieving the goals of the recommendations. Also it is oftentimes easier to achieve a consensus around ends rather than means. Parties asked to make changes are usually more willing to do so if they retain some control over how these changes will be realized* (Siegel and Tucker 1985, p. 316).

Further, researchers should make clear the connection between their recommendations and their data. To the extent that recommendations are perceived as politically based rather than data based, decision makers are less likely to use them.

Other researchers, however, have found that utilization was positively associated with reports that contained explicit recommendations for action—have, in fact, found a positive association between reports that challenge the status quo and utilization of research by decision makers (Weiss and Bucuvalas 1980).

Guba and Lincoln (1981) suggest one way to understand these different findings. Whereas Siegel and Tucker implicitly assume that researchers develop recommendations independently and then provide them to decision makers, Guba and Lincoln suggest that researchers develop recommendations in collaboration with decision makers. Under these circumstances, target audiences might more positively receive explicit recommendations for action or recommendations of a more fundamental nature.

Another approach to developing useful recommendations suggests that time constraints often force researchers to develop recommendations without a full consideration of the possible alternatives for action suggested by the data (Roberts-Gray, Buller, and Sparkman 1987). Rather than leave recommendations to the end of the research process, perhaps researchers should write recommendations during research design, using a "what if" approach.

> *By thinking at the beginning about recommendations that may be made at the close of the evaluation, the evaluator helps ensure that evaluation results will contribute to program improvement. . . . The logic linking data with action is spelled out and easy to trace . . . . It can show where additional data are needed and identify areas where data thought to be needed would be useless in fact* (Roberts-Gray, Buller, and Sparkman 1987, p. 681).

Report format

The format of the report is another factor related to utilization. Several researchers recommend that reports be organized around issues rather than methods (DeLoria and Brookins 1984; Ewell 1983; Forrest 1981; Kinnick 1985). Reports should directly address practitioners' concerns—which may require writing several reports or memos, each focusing on a different issue. Reports should be brief, avoid research jargon, and use graphics to summarize and display major findings (Forrest 1981; Guba and Lincoln 1981).

A set of useful recommendations about writing research reports for decision makers suggests that the traditional "dissertation-style" approach may be inconvenient for decision makers because "the details needed to answer a single policy question may be scattered across several chapters" (DeLoria and Brookins 1984, p. 648). The time and effort required to locate and integrate relevant information may deter use of the report.

As an alternative to the traditional approach, researchers should prepare two reports—one scientific and one policy (DeLoria and Brookins 1984). The latter would be brief, organized around major policy questions, and in the language of the practitioner. Reports that get used in decision making have the following characteristics:

1. *The questions addressed are clearly linked to real policy decisions.*
2. *At least some questions in each report consider the costs affecting policy.*

3. *Policy questions form the central organizing theme of the report.*
4. *The reports describe enough of the policy context to permit informed interpretation without outside sources.*
5. *Evaluation methodology is played down.*
6. *Reports begin with a brief summary of the essential findings.*
7. *Backup narrative for the executive summary is "chunked" into easily located, brief segments throughout the body of the report.*
8. *Only simple statistics are presented.*
9. *Where jargon is used, it is the jargon of the practitioners, not of the evaluators.*
10. *Concrete recommendations for action are based on specific findings* (DeLoria and Brookins 1984, pp. 660–62).

Within higher education, researchers must walk a fine line between turning off their audience by being too technical and turning off their audience by being too simplistic. Especially when professors trained in research will be reading the reports, detailed information about sampling, design, and analysis may be desirable to establish the validity of the methods employed. This technical information, however, should be provided in an appendix or self-contained chapter, with the most important information repeated in other sections that are devoted to major questions of research and policy.

Structures and settings

The ideal setting is one in which decision makers can jointly review and discuss the research data. Committees associated with the major campus issues provide opportunities for consideration of research findings and implementation of recommendations. Open forums could be held as well to encourage a broad range of students, faculty, and staff to discuss the findings. Or top administrators might sponsor a retreat for administrators to review the data and brainstorm about its implications for action.

Special events created specifically to consider the research on outcomes have the advantage of emphasizing administrative commitment to the project and of providing a setting in which the project is a primary (or exclusive) focus. On the other hand, when discussion of the findings is integrated into ongoing committees or task forces, the research on outcomes may come to be perceived as relevant to day-to-day decision making and an integral aspect of "management systems."

The importance of organizational factors can be summarized as follows:

> *One way of increasing the likelihood that student outcomes information will be used by decision makers is to put the information in a form suited to some of their regular activities. For most decision makers, student outcomes information falls into the category of "nice to know" rather than "need to know." Outcomes information is much more likely to be recognized as relevant if it is not seen as distinct from the kinds of productivity information upon which most decision makers claim to base their findings* (Ewell 1983, p. 48).

Barriers to Use

This section describes additional factors that hinder utilization.

Gap between researchers and practitioners

While researchers traditionally strive for objectivity and neutrality, advocacy is an important element in the administrative role. And while researchers may prefer complex methods and an extended time frame for data collection and analysis, decision makers require information that can be quickly obtained and easily assimilated. These and other differences between researchers and administrators may lead administrators to perceive research data as irrelevant in their decision making (cf. Caplan 1977; Siegel and Tucker 1985). One possible approach to this problem is for researchers to have the foresight to build data bases that ultimately will provide a resource for getting rapid and sophisticated answers to complex questions.

Although the goals of most colleges and universities include the support of research activities, administrators may fail to perceive these activities as useful in meeting their own needs for information. Therefore, the researcher must educate administrators about the potential benefits of research and must respond to the values, language, and goals of target audiences.

The institution's decentralized structure

The benefits of using data available on campus have been discussed in previous sections. This task may be rendered difficult when relevant data elements are located in different sites on campus and when the data are collected or processed in such a way that it is difficult to merge with other information (Kinnick 1985). Some additional expenses could be incurred as well if data must be recoded or rekeyed. Such problems can almost always be solved if sufficient time is allowed and if top administrators communicate the importance of the effort to those who manage the data.

Another problem can arise from the decentralized nature of the university: The decentralized structure of most schools means that no one office or department is responsible for student outcomes (Ewell 1983). Support from top administrators, especially incentives for collection or application of data about outcomes, can overcome this barrier.

Faculty resistance

Resistance from faculty is often cited as a reason that assessments of outcomes are inappropriate for a particular institution (Ewell 1985). Faculty may fear a negative evaluation or may believe that assessments of outcomes will not accurately measure the educational process. Recent research (Astin and Ayala 1987) suggests that resistance from faculty is a normal part of any attempt to implement such assessments. It is to be expected but it can be effectively dealt with. Barriers erected by faculty can be overcome by involving faculty in the research, by differentiating assessments of outcomes from teaching evaluations, and by using multiple measures to compensate for the limitations of individual instruments.

Cost

Even when decision makers believe in the value of such assessment, institutional research is one of many programs competing for limited funds and administrators may be unable or unwilling to financially support the research program. Again, support from top administrators and early education and involvement of key audiences increase the likelihood that the assessment will be funded. Costs can be reduced by using data already available on campus (Ewell 1985).

Timing and follow-through

Late delivery of research is among the most common reasons for data's underuse (Kinnick 1985). This situation should be avoided at all costs, because it not only reduces (or eliminates) the usefulness of the current project but also decreases the likelihood of decision makers' support for future projects.

Underuse may also result if the researcher fails to conduct any follow-up activities after the final report is released. Such activities may take many forms—releasing additional memos and analyses, requesting feedback from target audiences, or participating in implementation activities, for example. Without such activities, decision makers are likely to be distracted by other, more visible issues, and findings will be neglected.

Academic games

A number of "academic games" can be observed in committee meetings at most colleges—rationalization, passing the buck, obfuscation, co-optation, recitation, and displacement/projection (Astin 1976). One of the purposes of such games is to relieve committee members of responsibility for action; the games in this way act as barriers to utilization. Researchers can use both direct and indirect approaches to end the games and maintain control of the discussion.

Paradoxes of Guidelines for Utilization

Applying the information provided in this monograph poses several challenges, including reconciling recommendations that appear to be contradictory. This section briefly describes some of these apparent conflicts.

Rational versus irrational decision making

Applied research assumes that decision making is rational—that administrators assess situations, identify problems, generate and evaluate potential solutions, and implement the "best" alternative. In reality, however, decision making may proceed along highly subjective, unsystematic, and even irrational lines (McClintock 1984; Weick 1979; Weiss 1988). Under such circumstances "legitimating" uses of research may be more likely to occur than "instrumental" uses. Researchers must weigh the risks of their research being misrepresented or distorted against the risks of its being ignored altogether.

Involvement versus control

The emphasis of action research on involving target audiences in the research process may threaten the traditional objectivity and neutrality of researchers. As researchers try to understand and appeal to the values of decision makers, they risk "co-optation" (Dawson and D'Amico 1985). Similarly, the researcher walks a thin line between profiting from the involvement of decision makers and losing control of the project (Siegel and Tucker 1985). Opponents of a project might criticize the research as partisan if researchers have worked too closely with target audiences.

Democracy versus competition in decision making

The "democratic" decision-making process characteristic of action research may conflict with competitive norms found in many colleges (Buhl and Lindquist 1981). The participatory process recommended by most action researchers will be ineffective if decision making is perceived as a competitive situation in which one person wins and another loses. When such norms are firmly entrenched, the researcher must strive to create a safe setting for open discussion with target audiences.

Involvement versus timeliness

While the benefits of involving target audiences in the research have been discussed at length, it should be pointed out that such a process may significantly slow down the progress of the research. It takes time to schedule meetings, to consult with various stake holders, and to respond to their feedback. Further, most decision makers are very busy people who can invest only a limited amount of time in the effort. Because late delivery of data is a major barrier to utilization, the researcher must either be prepared to start the process early or balance time pressure against political pressure.

Methodological rigor versus time and cost

While comparative, longitudinal studies that conform to established standards of quasi-experimental design, use multiple measures, and supplement quantitative findings with qualitative data are desirable, they are also expensive and time consuming. The obvious rejoinder to this objection is that assessments that fail to accurately respond to the research questions are hard to justify, regardless of their cost or "efficiency." Researchers may have to decide which methodological tradeoffs are least damaging, however (cf. Cook and Campbell 1979).

Technical credibility versus readability

The brief reports recommended by many researchers (for example, Ewell 1983; Forrest 1981; Palola and Lehmann 1976) do not include room for detailed descriptions of research methods. Academic audiences, however, may be unwilling to accept the findings without such information. The additional bulk created by including this information, on the other hand, may deter decision makers from reading the report.

Researcher's objectivity versus advocacy
Action research places the researcher in the role of advocate as well as technician, although writers disagree about the most effective methods of advocacy (see the previous discussion on research recommendations). Institutional researchers must face another dilemma: If they act as advocates in one situation, might that limit their credibility in another? When researchers become politically active, will decision makers trust their information on a continuing basis? If researchers decide not to enter the political arena, however, will their data be misrepresented or neglected?

PRACTICAL SUGGESTIONS FOR CONDUCTING ASSESSMENTS

This chapter proposes a number of practical suggestions for implementing a comprehensive program of assessing outcomes.

In general, the authors recommend that researchers use a combination of established and locally designed instruments.

Be Informative Rather Than Adversarial

As suggested earlier, a program of institutional outcomes assessment is likely to be useful if it is based on a talent development approach to excellence rather than the traditional resource and reputational approaches, which are inherently competitive and therefore adversarial: Who has the brightest students? Who has the most prestigious faculty? Who has the largest library? This competitive approach is further reflected in the ways traditionally used to assess students: letter-grade averages, relativistic measures that pit students against each other. Students are thus tested and graded to determine whether they should be admitted, awarded credit, or permitted to graduate rather than to determine how much and how well they actually learn. This attitude also spills over into attempts to assess faculty members: Most assessments of faculty performance are designed to determine whether they should be hired, promoted, or given tenure. Under such conditions, the institution's assessment program is bound to be perceived as a threat. Further, this adversarial view of assessment tends to put students and faculty members into passive roles: Students and professors submit to assessment and try to show themselves in the most favorable light possible.

By contrast, the talent development concept and its associated notion of involvement demand a very different purpose for assessment. In this case, assessment is used primarily for feedback to increase the involvement of students and faculty members and to develop their talents as completely as possible. Such assessment is active rather than passive, as it is designed to facilitate and improve performance rather than merely to evaluate it. Furthermore, the information gathered is used to benefit the parties involved rather than to pass judgment on them.

Build on What You Already Have

The talent development approach to assessment does not necessarily require that institutions embark on an entirely new program of testing and evaluation. For example, most institutions already employ some kind of testing program for admissions, and many also use various types of placement tests. Under a talent development approach, these admissions and placement tests can be viewed as a kind of "pretest" for subsequent follow-up assessments ("posttests") that could provide a longitudinal measure of change or growth in students' competence. At the same time, upper-division competency tests in writing, basic academic skills, and related areas, which have become increasingly popular and have even been mandated in some public institutions, might provide an important "posttest" that could be "pretested" with the same or similar device at the time the student enters the institution. These pretests on upper-division competence, incidentally, can also be important guides for effective placement and counseling. Indeed, it may well be that pretesting students with upper-division tests of competence at the time of entry could replace currently used admissions or placement tests, thereby obviating the need for *any* increase in the amount of assessment.

But perhaps the most important existing assessments to be elaborated into a talent development context are classroom examinations. Most undergraduate courses involve some kind of final examination, and many also involve midterm examinations of various types. In most courses, these same (or parallel) exams could be given to the new student at the time of initial enrollment in the course, thereby providing a baseline against which to measure change in the midterm and final examinations. An important additional benefit from such pretesting in the classroom is that it gives students a very concrete idea of what is to be expected in the course and of how much growth the student must demonstrate to reach acceptable standards of performance.

Start Simply

For institutions that have not already established a tradition of comprehensive assessment, it is important to initiate any new outcomes assessment modestly with minimal disruption of institutional activities. A more comprehensive and complete system can evolve from these modest beginnings.

Institutions often resist comprehensive assessments of students' cognitive development because of their high costs and logistical problems. This resistance can be compounded by the fact that such assessments require a substantial lapse of time between pretest and posttest before any useful information on students' growth and development is obtained. One short cut that can provide useful information almost immediately is the use of so-called "surrogate" measures of students' cognitive development. Thus, questionnaires can be administered to students that involve three kinds of questions: (1) self-reports about how much students think they have actually improved their skills and knowledge in various areas (a kind of quick-and-dirty value-added assessment after the fact); (2) student ratings of a wide range of university experiences and services, including classroom teaching, counseling, residential facilities, and so forth; and (3) a "time diary" in which students provide information about their level of involvement in various activities by indicating how much time they spend on studying, discussing class subject matter with students and faculty, and so on. All three can be obtained from a single questionnaire administered to students at any time during their undergraduate years. The results of such assessments can be analyzed rapidly and disseminated to faculty, staff, students, and others who have an interest in the results. A national program that produced normative information on such matters is the Follow-Up Student Survey (FUSS) conducted by the Higher Education Research Institute at UCLA.

Develop a Data Base

As noted, it is important for an institution that does not have a well-established tradition of longitudinal student assessment to begin to develop such a system modestly. A minimally useful student data base should incorporate the following core elements:

1. *Successful completion of a program of study.* In its simplest form, this measure would involve a dichotomy: The student either completes a program or drops out. More sophisticated approaches to this measure would involve determining whether a student's undergraduate achievements are consistent with his or her degree plans at college entry.
2. *Cognitive development.* The basic purpose of this category of information is to determine whether the institution is achieving its basic instructional purpose: to develop its students' cognitive abilities. Again, the "surrogate" measure of longitudinal cognitive development—the student's self-report of learning in various subject areas—would seem to be a modest way to start. Ultimately, of course,

it would be important to incorporate actual assessments of pretest and posttest cognitive performance in areas that are relevant to the curricular program.

3. *Students' involvement and satisfaction.* Students' satisfaction with the institution's program is one of the most important indications of an institution's effectiveness. Students should be asked not only about their overall satisfaction but also about their satisfaction with more specific matters: the quality of teaching, advising, curriculum, facilities, extracurricular activities, and student services. Perhaps the best way to assess involvement, as suggested earlier, is to ask students to keep time diaries indicating how much time (per week, for example) they spend on various activities (studying, interacting with each other and with professors, working at an outside job, engaging in athletics and other activities, and so forth).

Be More Absolute, Less Relative

Almost all of the widely used aptitude and achievement tests in higher education follow a similar practice in test design and construction: A list of multiple-choice test items is developed and administered to a sample of students. The number of items answered correctly (possibly with adjustments for wrong answers) is calculated for each student and then converted into a derived measure, such as a standard score or a percentile score. This process of conversion basically wipes out the fundamental information about how many or what percent of questions the students answered correctly, which questions were answered correctly, and so on. Instead, it provides only relativistic information derived from the normal curve, that is, reflecting only how one student has performed relative to others.

While such relative measures are used almost universally in large-scale national and state examinations, they present some potentially serious problems. Besides indicating nothing about the student's *absolute* level of performance, such relativistic scores give no information about how difficult the items were or what the student's test performance implies about potential for performing well on the job, profiting from further education, and the like. More important, such relative measures offer no way of reflecting changes in the student's performance over a period of time. Thus, it is possible for a student's absolute (actual) level of performance or competence to improve considerably over a period of time, while his or her relative performance remains the same or even declines during the same period.

Measures of absolute performance can be developed from the types of multiple-choice items usually found in aptitude or achievement tests in several possible ways, but perhaps the most straightforward approach is simply to record the number of items answered correctly. Change or growth in the student's development can thus be assessed in terms of increases in the number or percentage of such items answered correctly. One useful elaboration of this approach is to develop expectancy tables that show the probability of various events (graduating on time, graduating with honors, performing well on the job, and so forth) as a function of the number of items correctly answered. Change or growth can then be measured in terms of increases in these probabilities over time.

Another method is to label particular points on the distribution of scores (whether they be raw or derived scores) in terms of the level of performance typical of that point. For example, if one were interested in using an outcome measure of writing skill to certify students for graduation, the lowest scores might indicate borderline literacy, and the highest scores might correspond to the level of writing competence required of students pursuing a doctoral-level graduate education. The significance of the scale points would be made even clearer if examples of actual items were used to show the most difficult types of items passed by the majority of people scoring at a particular point on the scale.

Get More from Your Standardized Tests

Given the heavy use of standardized tests by most colleges and universities, it is unfortunate that so little of the information collected in these tests is actually used for educational purposes to enhance students' talent development. One way to enhance the educational usefulness of such instruments is to obtain information concerning the student's *raw scores* as well as standardized or derived scores. Such information is readily available from the testing organizations and should be requested by all institutions that use these tests for admissions, placement, or other purposes.

Another potentially more important type of information is the students' performance on individual test *items*. If it were possible to know how students perform on individual items—which ones they find most difficult and which ones they find rela-

tively easy—such information could be invaluable in planning and evaluating the curriculum.

Testing companies have resisted providing information on performance on individual test items on the grounds that such information is "unreliable." This objection may be valid in the case of individual students, but it is not relevant to information that could be provided in *aggregate* form. That is, it would be extremely valuable to faculty members to know how a *group* of students performed on each test item. Again, testing organizations should be able to provide such information at relatively little additional cost.

Another objection to the provision of data on performance on individual test questions is the need to protect test security. This argument is really a weak one, given the theory underlying the construction of most achievement tests. Briefly, the items for such tests are selected from a hypothetical "domain" of all possible test questions that could be asked about the particular subject in question. If providing feedback on individual items to institutions violates the security of a particular set of items, then the test company can simply write new items each year. If the domain is finite, then once all possible test items have been written and made public, the test makers can sample randomly from this domain in constructing a new test each year. It might be argued that under these conditions professors will encourage their students to study for the test by learning the answers to all the items. But what is wrong with this approach? If a student knows the answers to all possible questions that could be asked about a particular body of knowledge, then that student knows, by definition, that body of knowledge.

By obtaining access to results for individual test questions on an instrument like the College Entrance Examination Board's SAT, institutions can then repeat some of these tests after one, two, or four years to measure improvement in students' performance on specific items. Moreover, if testing organizations could be persuaded to perform equating studies where various instruments such as the SAT and GRE are equated, the results of these tests could also be used to measure improvement in cognitive performance during the undergraduate years.

While such changes in testing organizations' feedback may be difficult for an individual institution to achieve, it should not be too difficult for several institutions that are members of regional associations or possibly public systems to join together to request such modifications from testing organizations. Under such pressure, a good likelihood exists that testing organizations will provide the requested data.

Combine the Use of Local Assessment Instruments and Standardized Instruments

Even though test development can be an expensive exercise, locally designed tests can often provide information with most relevance to practitioners (Baird 1976). An important advantage of locally designed assessments is the "ownership" that comes from the involvement of faculty and staff in development, especially true in the case of departmental comprehensive examinations in the major, which presumably cover the subject matter closest to the hearts of the faculty.

Nationally developed instruments generally have the advantage of established reliability and validity. In many cases, national norms are available, providing additional opportunities for comparison. Longitudinal trends may be available as well, providing information about change over time in students' capabilities.

The decision about whether to design one's own instrument or use an already existing one cannot be made independently of the goals for assessment. If the goal of the assessment is to satisfy concerns about accountability for an external review, use of an already existing instrument would probably be most appropriate. The established validity of the test would lend legitimacy to the assessment, and the opportunity to compare institutional results against national norms might be particularly important. On the other hand, outcomes assessments for institutional self-improvement might require specific information that an established instrument is unable to provide.

In general, the authors recommend that researchers use a combination of established and locally designed instruments. The former are often already available on campus (for example, SAT and GRE scores and placement tests). This information could be supplemented with additional data derived from surveys tailored to the research questions.

Exchanging and sharing locally designed instruments among institutions offer several advantages. First, a better quality instrument is obtained because the researcher can benefit from the experience of colleagues at other schools. Psychometric information can be obtained from the institution that originally developed and used the instrument. Second, some comparative data may be obtained if institutions are willing to share their findings.

Be Opportunistic

The practical problems involved in large-scale institutional assessment of students' competence are not to be underestimated. The time of students and faculty members is at a premium in most institutions, and any additional assessments that would be required to implement the talent development approach should be incorporated with minimal intrusion on the time and energy of faculty and students.

Many institutions fail to realize that once students begin to attend classes it may be extremely difficult to find a way to conduct pretest assessments. It is important to realize that the student who is in the process of matriculating for the first time is generally in an extremely cooperative frame of mind and therefore an ideal subject for pretest or placement assessments. It thus makes good sense to capitalize on this opportunity as fully as possible and to include as many assessments as might be needed for a full-fledged program. Follow-up assessments are almost inevitably more difficult, as students may never again congregate in a single place at the same time and in the same cooperative frame of mind. Some institutions may well find it necessary to mandate follow-up posttest assessments. In those states where some kind of mandatory upper-division competency assessment (such as the writing requirement at the California State University) is already in place, then this posttest assessment might also be seen as an occasion to include other posttests where appropriate. In short, institutions should attempt to identify those points in the students' institutional experience where assessments are likely to be least intrusive and most acceptable to the larger academic community.

Use Gentle Persuasion

As already noted, follow-up assessments of cognitive outcomes are frequently difficult to conduct if they are not mandated by external agencies or by institutional policy. Requiring all students to participate in outcomes assessments has several obvious advantages. First, the risk of distorting findings because of a biased sample is minimized. Second, more statistical power is gained in analyses of results from the larger number of respondents. Voluntary participation in the testing may lead to a large amount of attrition from the project (in addition to attrition from the institution) that can substantially reduce the size of a posttest sample. Finally, required participation of all students avoids issues of equity that may be encountered if some but not all students are asked to invest their time in the project.

On the other hand, required participation raises both logistical and ethical issues. While pretesting can be implemented relatively easily during freshman orientation, it may be difficult and expensive to schedule posttesting sessions for all students in a cohort. Further, administrators and faculty may question the desirability of required testing if the benefits of outcomes assessments have not yet been unambiguously demonstrated. And students may object to forced participation in posttesting on grounds ranging from lack of time to invasion of privacy.

When the institutional environment does not favor required outcomes assessments, researchers can choose among many strategies for increasing voluntary participation:

- educating students about the benefits that will accrue to them as a result of their participation;
- appealing to students' sense of citizenship or educating them about the benefits that will accrue to subsequent classes as a result of their participation;
- providing incentives for groups or individuals to participate (positive reinforcement); or
- offering release from some other responsibility in exchange for participation (negative reinforcement).

The best results might be obtained from a combination of these approaches. Educative approaches typically emphasize either applying the research findings to institutional self-improvement or providing individual students with their own scores and/or aggregated results as a means of increasing insight into their own development. Where feasible, students might also be offered counseling to aid in interpreting and applying the results of test scores.

Possible incentives include a broad range of rewards for participation. Among those that some institutions have used are cash prizes, a chance to win a larger prize in a random drawing of participants, discounts on campus services, tickets to cultural events, and T-shirts. Student groups might also be invited to compete for some prize, awarded to the group with the largest number of participants in the testing. Students' participation can also be obtained by allowing students to substitute participation in the outcomes assessment for some other required task.

In the short run, incentives are most effective in obtaining participation. Educative appeals may be more effective in ensuring a sufficient posttest sample, however. If students find the incentive for the pretest inadequate compensation for their participation, they are unlikely to return for follow-up testing.

Involve Faculty from the Start

Several benefits are obtained by including key faculty members in all stages of the research. First, faculty can serve as technical consultants to the research project. For example, they can be asked to develop or review assessment instruments, and they can offer guidance on research design and analysis of outcomes assessments. In this context, faculty provide a pool of experts from which practitioners may draw specialized assistance in conducting an outcomes assessment.

A second benefit is that faculty support will increase when opinion leaders are actively engaged in the project. Practitioners will be better able to respond to faculty concerns about outcomes assessment when such concerns are expressed at the earliest stages of the project. And faculty are less likely to resist a project to which they have made substantial contributions.

For example, faculty commonly resist outcomes assessments because they believe that the assessment instruments fail to appropriately define the major concepts and methods of their disciplines. Under such circumstances, faculty could be invited to design their own assessment instrument for measuring students' competence. This approach both increases the validity of the research instruments and reduces faculty objections to the project.

Finally, active involvement of faculty will reduce concerns that such evaluations will be used punitively—either to identify "bad" teachers or to weed out "bad" students. Their participation on the project will reinforce administrators' promises that the evaluation will not be used in such ways.

CONCLUSION

Summary and Review

We have discussed the potential of student outcomes research to inform decision making and thereby improve postsecondary education. We have pondered the reasons for the frequent failure of outcomes assessments to realize this potential. We believe that we can do better in the future. To this end, we have described a variety of approaches to and instruments for assessment and have provided suggestions for ensuring that outcomes assessments will be both methodologically sound and relevant to the interests of institutional leaders and decision makers. We have further suggested that the talent development perspective provides a theoretical perspective and a methodological framework that enhances the usefulness of outcomes data for improving postsecondary education.

The authors will develop an information base that will greatly increase the validity and cost effectiveness of assessment.

The reaction of researchers and practitioners in higher education to the oft-heard call for longitudinal assessment is frequently a resounding "yes, but." It is difficult, especially in today's educational climate, to be "against assessment," but we can all recite a growing number of reasons that we have heard for why assessment is ill advised within a particular institution at the present time (cf. Ewell 1984):

- It's impossible to measure what really matters to us.
- We don't have the time or the money to implement these ideas.
- We don't want our faculty to "teach the test."
- The state/administration/other would misuse the information.
- We'd never get our students to cooperate.
- We'd never get support from the leadership of this institution.
- We'd never get the faculty to cooperate.

It would be a mistake to dismiss them as convenient excuses for avoiding the technical and practical challenges of assessment. In fact, each concern highlights important issues for consideration in planning a talent development assessment program. Effective assessment programs require that conceptual, methodological, and political issues be addressed. To assist readers in determining their readiness to implement assessment programs and to briefly review the material presented in this monograph, the following quick "self-study" guide is offered:

1. Has this institution identified its primary goals for an outcomes assessment? Is the assessment primarily to satisfy external demands for accountability or to promote institutional self-improvement? What is the institution's commitment to a program of longitudinal assessment of student development?
2. Has this institution developed a coherent philosophy of institutional mission? Do faculty, administrators, and students share a concept of "excellence" that can be used to establish more specific educational goals and policies?
3. Based on the educational philosophy, mission, and goals of the institution, what outcomes are most important to assess? Has the institution developed operational definitions for these outcomes?
4. What standardized instruments are currently administered to students for placement, diagnosis, or evaluation? Can these tests be readministered to obtain useful information about students' growth and development?
5. In addition to those currently in use, are other standardized instruments available to measure outcomes of interest? If so, do test vendors define the concepts measured in a manner that is congruent with the goals and interests of the institution?
6. What are the trade-offs within this institution in using standardized instruments (if available) versus developing assessment tools internally? How can these approaches be combined?
7. How can the assessment program best complement and extend ongoing efforts at assessment within the institution, such as placement tests or upper-division competency tests?
8. For any particular instrument under consideration, are students likely to bottom out on the pretest or top out on the posttest? Are scores available on individual items as well as for total scores? Are individual scores valid in addition to aggregate scores? Are absolute measures of performance available in addition to relativistic measures of performance? Do the instruments have established reliability and validity? Are longitudinal or cross-

sectional comparisons available or potentially available? If instruments are commercially available, do vendors provide space for optional, locally designed questions?

9. Is the institution prepared to administer the assessment instruments within the framework of accepted standards of field research (quasi-experimental design)? That is, has the institution identified and secured the cooperation of appropriate comparison groups? Is the institution committed to a design using pretests and posttests? Which potential threats to internal and external validity are of most concern, and how might these threats be minimized?
10. Should students' participation in the assessment program be required or voluntary? If voluntary, how might students' compliance be secured for both the pretest and the posttest? How might voluntary participation influence the external validity of the assessment?
11. What possible side effects of assessment for students should be anticipated (for example, psychological distress associated with bottoming out)? When are the most advantageous times to administer student assessments?
12. Has the research team secured the involvement and support of key stake holders and target audiences (from faculty, administrators, staff, and students) at all phases of the project? Do top administrators support the assessment? Are they committed to using results of assessment in evaluation, curriculum or program development, planning and policy development, or other forms of decision making? What reasons might faculty, administrators, or students provide for delaying or discounting the assessment program? Has the research team responded appropriately to these concerns and involved potential critics in the planning process?
13. Is the research team prepared to complete assessment and analysis expeditiously and provide specialized, issue-based research reports or presentations that respond directly to the needs of target audiences?
14. Is it advisable for the research team to provide recommendations? If so, what approaches will ensure that the recommendations are closely linked to the data and that decision makers will consider them seriously?
15. How can assessment data be integrated into a student data base that includes elements related to successful

completion of a program of study, cognitive development, and the involvement and satisfaction of students?

Recommendations for Future Research

As more institutions initiate longitudinal assessment programs, either on their own initiative or in response to external mandates and incentives, the authors will develop an information base that will greatly increase the validity and cost effectiveness of assessment. In the meantime, it is necessary to continue conducting research and analysis directed at a number of gaps in existing knowledge. The following recommendations for future research are therefore offered:

1. The scarcity of standardized instruments that respond to institutional needs and goals in cognitive assessment has been widely recognized (cf. Banta and Fisher 1987; Boyer 1987; Edgarton 1987). Those standardized instruments that are designed to measure a broad range of "higher order" skills and processes (postsecondary-level analytic, communication, and critical thinking abilities, for example) are often expensive and difficult to administer. While we applaud such innovative efforts as the ACT COMP, the McBer Behavioral Event Interview, and the ETS Academic Profile, a continuing need clearly is test development for the measurement of cognitive skills and abilities.

2. We strongly encourage those institutions who have used or plan to use the instruments reviewed here (or others) to publish or present their experiences so that we can develop a pool of knowledge about the tools most appropriate for talent development assessments. Systematic comparisons of alternative instruments designed to measure similar outcomes are also needed. Such comparisons would ideally examine such factors as the manner in which the tests define the concepts under investigation, test reliability and validity (including both convergent and discriminant validity), the suitability of the instruments for talent development approaches, practical issues in administering and scoring tests, faculty and student attitudes toward the instruments, and usefulness of the results for institutional planning and decision making.

3. Because of the limitations of standardized tests, institutions will undoubtedly continue to design their own assessment tools to supplement if not replace commercially available instruments. Instruments such as the ETS Academic Profile and the CIRP Freshman and Follow-up Student Surveys that pro-

vide space for optional, locally designed questions provide one approach to combining the best of standardized and locally designed assessments. For those institutions that want to develop their own assessment instruments, however, especially to measure students' cognitive development, a guide to test development in this area would be most helpful. A comprehensive "how to" guide, geared to the needs of institutional researchers and managers would offer a useful resource that would significantly improve the quality and cost effectiveness of local assessment.

4. Prospective, longitudinal, multi-institutional studies conforming to accepted standards of quasi-experimental design continue to be sorely lacking in the literature, especially when the focus is college students' cognitive development. Multi-institutional studies are essential to support analyses that investigate the additive or interactive effects on student development of institutional characteristics, student characteristics, educational curricula or programs, and student support services and co-curricular programs. Such analyses are needed to indicate the factors that promote learning within particular environments or for particular types of students. They will also point to the extent to which trends and patterns observed in one environment can be generalized to other settings and populations. Multi-institutional studies also offer an opportunity to increase statistical power and thereby compare subgroups of students that are usually too small to yield valid data within single-institution studies.

5. Typically, research about outcomes addresses cognitive and affective outcomes separately, as if they were independent phenomena. We encourage the development of more integrative approaches, considering the reciprocal relations between cognitive and affective factors. Similarly, studies that link levels of performance on tests of cognitive abilities to concrete behavioral outcomes (for example, graduation or enrollment in graduate or professional school) would be helpful for deriving additional benefits from assessment.

6. Although both researchers and practitioners are increasingly finding effective means to use information about outcomes in decision making, the need for additional attention to the broad issue of utilization continues. Future research might review literature in other applied fields, such as planning, public policy, and environmental psychology, to determine additional strategies for influencing decision making. Further,

although numerous researchers and practitioners.have reminded us that information about outcomes can be used in many different ways, we often still conclude that our research is underused if it does not contribute in a direct, linear, and observable manner to decision making. To help us move beyond this myth, development of a taxonomy of types of utilization, including common indicators of each type, could aid efforts to determine whether or how research and information about outcomes play a role in decision making. Finally, much of the higher education research on this issue is based on small sample sizes. Larger-scale surveys that assess factors associated with utilization at a large number of institutions would contribute to an understanding of this issue.

7. A final, perhaps naive, suggestion is that outcomes researchers develop more cooperative relationships with their colleagues. We rarely take the trouble to share details of our failures and successes with others. As a consequence, we lose the opportunity to observe or to influence the manner in which practitioners use data about outcomes at other than our own institutions. To learn from our failures and share our successes will require us to be less competitive and to develop a stronger sense of mutual trust. We hope, in short, that researchers will be willing to adopt a cooperative rather than adversarial approach to the evaluation of outcomes, not only in their relationships to the subjects of evaluation but also in their relationships with one another.

APPENDIX A

SUMMARY OF COGNITIVE ASSESSMENT INSTRUMENTS DISCUSSED

GENERAL EDUCATION TESTS

Instruments Geared toward Lower-Division Students

The ACT Assessment Program
American College Testing Program
2201 N. Dodge Street
P.O. Box 168
Iowa City, IA 52243
(319) 337-1000
195 minutes

Scholastic Aptitude Test and Test of Standard Written English
The College Board
45 Columbus Avenue
New York, NY 10023
(212) 713-8000
150 minutes and 30 minutes, respectively

General Examinations of the College-Level Examination Program
The College Board
5 general tests, 90 minutes each

Sequential Tests of Educational Progress, Series III
CTB/McGraw-Hill
Publishers Test Service
Del Monte Research Park
2500 Garden Road
Monterey, CA 93940
(800) 538-9547
5 tests, 40 minutes each

Stanford Test of Academic Skills (1982 Edition)
The Psychological Corporation
555 Academic Court
San Antonio, TX 78204
(512) 299-1061
135 minutes

Instruments Geared toward Upper-Division Students

Graduate Record Exam General Test
Educational Testing Service
Rosedale Road
Princeton, NJ 08541
(609) 921-9000
210 minutes

Academic Profile
Educational Testing Service
60 minutes *or* 180 minutes with optional 45-minute essay

Graduate Management Admissions Test
Educational Testing Service
240 minutes

Medical College Admission Test
Association of American Medical Colleges
One Dupont Circle, NW
Suite 200
Washington, DC 20036
(202) 828-0400
390 minutes

Law School Admission Test
Law School Admission Council
P.O. Box 2000
Newtown, PA 18940
(215) 968-1001
210 minutes

NTE Core Battery
Educational Testing Service
3 tests, 120 minutes each

NTE Pre-Professional Skills Test
Educational Testing Service
3 tests, 30 to 50 minutes each

Instruments Geared toward All Levels
College Outcomes Measures Project
American College Testing Program
360 minutes (composite) *or* less than 180 minutes (objective)

McBer Behavioral Event Interview
Council for Adult and Experiential Learning
10840 Little Patuxent Parkway
Columbia, MD 21044
(301) 997-3535
Varies

SPECIFIC SKILLS TESTS
Instruments Geared toward Lower-Division Students
English Composition Test with Essay
The College Board
60 minutes

Nelson-Denny Reading Test, Forms E and F
Riverside Publishing Company
8420 Bryn Mawr Avenue
Chicago, IL 60631
(800) 323-9540
35 minutes

Writing Proficiency Program
CTB/McGraw-Hill
30 to 50 minutes for multiple choice; 30 to 50 minutes per essay

Instruments Geared toward Upper-Division Students
Western Michigan English Qualifying Examination
Bernadine Carlson
% Western Michigan University
720 Sprau Tower
Kalamazoo, MI 49008
100 minutes

Doppelt Mathematical Reasoning Test
The Psychological Corporation
50 minutes

Miller Analogies Test
The Psychological Corporation
50 minutes

Instruments Geared toward All Levels
Watson-Glaser Critical Thinking Appraisal, Forms A and B
The Psychological Corporation
50 minutes

Cornell Critical Thinking Test, Level Z
Midwest Publications
P.O. Box 448
Pacific Grove, CA 93950
(408) 375-2455
50 minutes

Goyer Organization of Ideas Test, Form S
Robert S. Goyer
Department of Communication
Arizona State University
Tempe, AZ 85287
(602) 965-5095
40 to 60 minutes

SUBJECT MATTER COMPETENCY TESTS

Instruments Geared toward Lower-Division Students

Advanced Placement Program of the College Entrance Examination Board
The College Board
26 tests, up to 180 minutes each

College Board Achievement Tests
The College Board
14 tests, 60 minutes each

Instruments Geared toward Upper-Division Students

Graduate Record Exam Subject Tests
Educational Testing Service
17 tests, 170 minutes each

National Teacher Examination Specialty Area Tests
Educational Testing Service
26 tests, 120 minutes each

Instruments Geared toward All Levels

ACT Proficiency Examination Program
American College Testing Program
49 tests, 180 to 420 minutes each

College-Level Examination Program Subject Examinations
The College Board
46 tests, 90 minutes each

Cooperative Examination Program of the American Chemical Society
American Chemical Society
1155 Sixteenth Street, NW
Washington, DC 20036
(202) 872-4600
55 minutes

REFERENCES

The Educational Resources Information Center (ERIC) Clearinghouse on Higher Education abstracts and indexes the current literature on higher education for inclusion in ERIC's data base and announcement in ERIC's monthly bibliographic journal, *Resources in Education* (RIE). Most of these publications are available through the ERIC Document Reproduction Service (EDRS). For publications cited in this bibliography that are available from EDRS, ordering number and price are included. Readers who wish to order a publication should write to the ERIC Document Reproduction Service, 3900 Wheeler Avenue, Alexandria, Virginia 22304. (Phone orders with VISA or MasterCard are taken at 800/227-ERIC or 703/823-0500.) When ordering, please specify the document (ED) number. Documents are available as noted in microfiche (MF) and paper copy (PC). Because prices are subject to change, it is advisable to check the latest issue of *Resources in Education* for current cost based on the number of pages in the publication.

Aiken, Lewis R. 1985. "Review of the ACT Assessment Program." In *The Ninth Mental Measurements Yearbook*, edited by James V. Mitchell, Jr. Lincoln, Neb.: University of Nebraska–Lincoln, Buros Institute of Mental Measurements.

Allen, Louis A. 1982. *Making Managerial Planning More Effective*. New York: McGraw-Hill.

Alverno College Faculty. 1985. *Assessment at Alverno College*. Liberal Learning at Alverno Series. Milwaukee, Wis.: Alverno Productions.

Astin, Alexander W. Summer 1970. "The Methodology of Research on College Impact." Parts 1 and 2. *Sociology of Education* 43: 223–54+.

———. Spring 1974. "Measuring the Outcomes of Higher Education." In *Evaluating Institutions for Accountability*, edited by Howard R. Bowen. New Directions for Institutional Research No. 1. San Francisco: Jossey-Bass.

———. 1975. *Preventing Students from Dropping Out*. San Francisco: Jossey-Bass.

———. 1976. *Academic Gamesmanship: Student-Oriented Change in Higher Education*. New York: Praeger Publishers.

———. 1977. *Four Critical Years: Effects of College on Beliefs, Attitudes, and Knowledge*. San Francisco: Jossey-Bass.

———. 1985. *Achieving Institutional Excellence*. San Francisco: Jossey-Bass.

Astin, Alexander W., and Ayala, Frank, Jr. Summer 1987. "Institutional Strategies: A Consortial Approach to Assessment." *Educational Record* 68: 47–51.

Astin, Alexander W.; Henson, J.W.; and Christian, C.E. 1978. "The

Impact of Student Financial Aid Programs on Student Choice." Los Angeles: Higher Education Research Institute. ED 187 268. 568 pp. MF–$1.23; PC–$49.32.

Astin, Alexander W.; Inouye, Carolyn J.; and Korn, William S. 1986. *Evaluation of the CAEL Student Potential Program*. Los Angeles: University of California at Los Angeles, Higher Education Research Institute.

Astin, Alexander W., and Scherrei, Rita A. 1980. *Maximizing Leadership Effectiveness: Impact of Administrative Style on Faculty and Students*. San Francisco: Jossey-Bass.

Baird, Leonard I. Winter 1976. "Structuring the Environment to Improve Outcomes." In *Improving Educational Outcomes*, edited by Oscar Lenning. New Directions for Higher Education No. 16. San Francisco: Jossey-Bass.

Baldridge, J. Victor. 1983. "Strategic Planning in Higher Education: Does the Emperor Have Any Clothes?" In *The Dynamics of Organizational Change in Education,* edited by J. Victor Baldridge. Berkeley, Cal.: McCutchan Publishing Corp.

Banta, Trudy W., and Fisher, Homer S. 4 March 1987. "Measuring How Much Students Have Learned Entails Much More Than Simply Testing Them." *Chronicle of Higher Education* 33(25): 45.

Bauernfeind, Robert H. 1987. "Pre-Professional Skills Test." In *Test Critiques*, edited by Daniel J. Keyser and Richard C. Sweetland. Kansas City, Mo.: Test Corporation of America.

Berger, Allen. 1985. "Review of the Watson-Glaser Critical Thinking Appraisal." In *The Ninth Mental Measurements Yearbook*, edited by James V. Mitchell, Jr. Lincoln, Neb.: University of Nebraska–Lincoln, Buros Institute of Mental Measurements.

Bowen, Howard R. 1974a. "Accountability: Some Concluding Comments." In *Evaluating Institutions for Accountability*, edited by Howard R. Bowen. New Directions for Institutional Research No. 1. San Francisco: Jossey-Bass.

———. 1974b. "The Products of Higher Education." In *Evaluating Institutions for Accountability*, edited by Howard R. Bowen. New Directions for Institutional Research No. 1. San Francisco: Jossey-Bass.

———. Autumn 1977. "Outcome Data and Educational Decision Making." In *Appraising Information Needs of Decision Makers*, edited by Carl R. Adams. New Directions for Institutional Research No. 15. San Francisco: Jossey-Bass.

———. 1980. *Investment in Learning*. San Francisco: Jossey-Bass.

Boyer, Ernest L. 1987. *College: The Undergraduate Experience in America*. New York: Harper & Row.

Brown, Ric. 1985. "Review of Goyer Organization of Ideas Test." In *The Ninth Mental Measurements Yearbook*, edited by James V.

Mitchell, Jr. Lincoln, Neb.: University of Nebraska–Lincoln, Buros Institute of Mental Measurements.

Buhl, Lance C., and Lindquist, Jack. 1981. "Academic Improvement through Action Research." In *Increasing the Utilization of Institutional Research*, edited by Jack Lindquist. New Directions for Institutional Research No. 32. San Francisco: Jossey-Bass.

Buros, Oscar K., ed. 1965. *The Sixth Mental Measurements Yearbook*. Highland Park, N. J.: Gryphon Press.

———, ed. 1978. *The Eighth Mental Measurements Yearbook*. Highland Park, N. J.: Gryphon Press.

Campbell, Donald T. 1984. "Can We Be Scientific in Applied Social Science?" In *Evaluation Studies Review Annual Volume 9*, edited by Ross Conner. Beverly Hills, Cal: Sage Publishers.

Caplan, N. 1977. "A Minimal Set of Conditions Necessary for the Utilization of Social Science Knowledge in Policy Formation at the National Level." In *Using Social Research in Policy Making*, edited by Carol Weiss. Lexington, Mass.: Lexington Books.

Ciarlo, James A. 1981. *Utilizing Evaluation: Concepts and Measurement Techniques*. Beverly Hills, Cal.: Sage Publishers.

Clemens, W.V. 1965. "Doppelt Mathematical Reasoning Test." A review in *The Sixth Mental Measurements Yearbook*, edited by Oscar K. Buros. Highland Park, N. J.: Gryphon Press.

Cohn, Sanford J. 1985. "Review of Graduate Record Examination." In *The Ninth Mental Measurements Yearbook*, edited by James V. Mitchell, Jr. Lincoln, Neb.: University of Nebraska–Lincoln, Buros Institute of Mental Measurements.

Cook, Thomas D., and Campbell, Donald T. 1979. *Quasi-Experimentation: Design and Analysis Issues for Field Settings*. Chicago: Rand McNally Publishing Co.

Cronbach, Lee J., and Associates. 1980. *Toward Reform of Program Evaluation*. San Francisco: Jossey-Bass.

Crosby, Lawrence A. 1985. "Review of the Graduate Management Admission Test." In *The Ninth Mental Measurements Yearbook*, edited by James V. Mitchell, Jr. Lincoln, Neb.: University of Nebraska–Lincoln, Buros Institute of Mental Measurements.

Dawson, Judith, and D'Amico, Joseph. 1985. "Involving Program Staff in Evaluation Studies: A Strategy for Increasing Information Use and Enriching the Data Base." *Evaluation Review* 9: 173–88.

DeLoria, Dennis, and Brookins, G.K. 1984. "The Evaluation Report: A Weak Link to Policy." In *Evaluation Studies Review Annual Volume 9*, edited by Ross Conner. Beverly Hills, Cal.: Sage Publishers.

Deshler, David. 1984. *Evaluation for Program Improvement.* San Francisco: Jossey-Bass.

Dressel, Paul L. 1978. "Review of College-Level Examination Program." In *The Eighth Mental Measurements Yearbook*, edited by Oscar K. Buros. Highland Park, N. J.: Gryphon Press.

Edgarton, Russell. 1987. "An Assessment of Assessment." In *Assessing the Outcomes of Higher Education*. Proceedings of the 1986 ETS Invitational Conference. Princeton, N. J.: Educational Testing Service.

Educational Testing Service. November 1980. *College-Level Achievement Tests*. Princeton, N.J.: Author.

———. 1986. *ETS Test Collection Catalog*. Vol. 1, *Achievement Tests and Measurement Devices*. Phoenix, Ariz.: Oryx Press.

———. 1987. *The Academic Profile*. Princeton, N.J.: Author.

El-Khawas, Elaine, 1987. *Campus Trends, 1987*. Higher Education Panel Report No. 75. Washington, D.C.: American Council on Education.

Ewell, Peter T. 1983. *Information on Student Outcomes: How to Get It and How to Use It*. Boulder, Colo.: NCHEMS. ED 246 827. 89 pp. MF–$1.07; PC–$10.13.

———. 1984. *Toward the Self-Regarding Institution: Excellence and Accountability in Postsecondary Education*. Boulder, Colo.: NCHEMS.

———. 1985. "Some Implications for Practice." In *Assessing Education Outcomes*, edited by Peter T. Ewell. New Directions for Institutional Research No. 47. San Francisco: Jossey-Bass.

Feldman, Kenneth A., and Newcomb, T.M. 1969. *The Impact of College on Students*. San Francisco: Jossey-Bass.

Fincher, Cameron. 1985. "What Is Value-Added Education?" *Research in Higher Education* 22: 395–98.

Floden, Robert. 1985. "Review of the Sequential Tests of Educational Progress." In *The Ninth Mental Measurements Yearbook*, edited by James V. Mitchell, Jr. Lincoln, Neb.: University of Nebraska–Lincoln, Buros Institute of Mental Measurements.

Forrest, Aubrey. 1981. "Outcome Evaluation for Revitalizing General Education." In *Increasing the Utilization of Institutional Research*, edited by Jack Lindquist. New Directions for Institutional Research No. 32. San Francisco: Jossey-Bass.

Forrest, A., and Steele, J. 1982. *Defining and Measuring General Education, Knowledge, and Skills*. Technical Report 1976–81. Iowa City: American College Testing Program.

Frary, Robert B. 1985. "Review of Goyer Organization of Ideas Test." In *The Ninth Mental Measurements Yearbook*, edited by James V. Mitchell, Jr. Lincoln, Neb.: University of Nebraska–Lincoln, Buros Institute of Mental Measurements.

Freeman, Howard E., and Solomon, Marian A. "Introduction: Evaluation and the Uncertain 80s." In *Evaluation Studies Review*

Annual Volume 6, edited by Howard Freeman and Marian Solomon. Beverly Hills, Cal.: Sage Publishers.

Geisinger, Kurt. 1987. "Miller Analogies Test." In *Test Critiques*, edited by Daniel J. Keyser and Richard C. Sweetland. Kansas City, Mo.: Test Corporation of America.

Grobstein, Clifford. 1984. "Should Imperfect Data Be Used to Guide Public Policy?" In *Evaluation Studies Review Annual Volume 9*, edited by Ross Conner. Beverly Hills, Cal.: Sage Publishers.

Guba, Egon G., and Lincoln, Yvonna S. 1981. *Effective Evaluation*. San Francisco: Jossey-Bass.

Hambleton, Ronald K. 1987. "Nelson-Denny Reading Test, Forms E & F." In *Test Critiques*, edited by Daniel J. Keyser and Richard C. Sweetland. Kansas City, Mo.: Test Corporation of America.

Helmstadter, Gerald C. 1985. "Review of Watson-Glaser Critical Thinking Appraisal." In *The Ninth Mental Measurements Yearbook*, edited by James V. Mitchell, Jr. Lincoln, Neb.: University of Nebraska–Lincoln, Buros Institute of Mental Measurements.

Humphreys, Lloyd G. 1965. "Miller Analogies Test." A review in *The Sixth Mental Measurements Yearbook*, edited by Oscar K. Buros. Highland Park, N. J.: Gryphon Press.

Kean College of New Jersey Presidential Task Force on Student Learning and Development. 1986. *A Proposal for Program Assessment at Kean College of New Jersey: Final Report of the Presidential Task Force on Student Learning and Development*. Union, N. J.: Kean College of New Jersey.

Kerlinger, Fred N. 1973. *Foundations of Behavioral Research*. 2d ed. New York: Holt, Rinehart & Winston.

Keyser, Daniel J., and Sweetland, Richard C., eds. 1987. *Test Critiques*. Kansas City, Mo.: Test Corporation of America.

Kifer, Edward. 1985. "Review of ACT Assessment Program." In *The Ninth Mental Measurements Yearbook*, edited by James V. Mitchell, Jr. Lincoln, Neb.: University of Nebraska–Lincoln, Buros Institute of Mental Measurements.

Kinnick, Mary K. 1985. "Increasing the Use of Student Outcomes Information." In *Assessing Education Outcomes*, edited by Peter T. Ewell. New Directions for Institutional Research No. 47. San Francisco: Jossey-Bass.

Knorr, Karin D. 1977. "Policymakers' Use of Social Science Knowledge: Symbolic or Instrumental?" In *Using Social Research in Public Policy Making*, edited by Carol Weiss. Lexington, Mass.: Lexington Books.

Kotler, Philip. 1982. *Marketing for Nonprofit Organizations*. Englewood Cliffs, N.J.: Prentice-Hall.

Lenning, Oscar T. 1980. "Needs as a Basis for Academic Program Planning." In *Academic Planning for the 1980s,* edited by Richard

B. Heydinger. New Directions for Institutional Research No. 28. San Francisco: Jossey-Bass.

Lenning, Oscar T., and Associates. 1977. *A Structure for the Outcomes of Postsecondary Education*. Boulder, Colo.: National Center for Higher Education Management Systems. ED 150 904. 86 pp. MF–$1.07; PC–$10.13.

Lindquist, Jack. 1981. "Quick, Dirty, and Useful." In *Increasing the Utilization of Institutional Research*, edited by Jack Lindquist. New Directions for Institutional Research No. 32. San Francisco: Jossey-Bass.

McClain, Charles J., and Krueger, Darrell W. 1985. "Using Outcomes Assessment: A Case Study in Institutional Change." In *Assessing Education Outcomes*, edited by Peter T. Ewell. New Directions for Institutional Research No. 47. San Francisco: Jossey-Bass.

McClintock, Charles. 1984. "Toward a Theory of Formative Program Evaluation." In *Evaluation for Program Improvement*, edited by D. Deshler. New Directions for Continuing Education No. 24. San Francisco: Jossey-Bass.

Melton, Gary B. 1985. "Review of Law School Admission Test." In *The Ninth Mental Measurements Yearbook*, edited by James V. Mitchell, Jr. Lincoln, Neb.: University of Nebraska–Lincoln, Buros Institute of Mental Measurements.

Mentkowski, Marcia, and Doherty, A. 1983. "Careering after College: Establishing the Validity of Abilities Learned in College for Later Careering and Professional Performance." Final Report to NIE. ED 252 144. 228 pp. MF–$1.07; PC–$22.60.

———. February 1984. "Abilities That Last a Lifetime: Outcomes of the Alverno Experience." *AAHE Bulletin* 36: 5–14.

Mentkowski, Marcia, and Loacker, Georgine. 1985. "Assessing and Validating the Outcomes of College." In *Assessing Education Outcomes*, edited by Peter T. Ewell. New Directions for Institutional Research No. 47. San Francisco: Jossey-Bass.

Mills, Edward. 1983. "Determining the Economic Returns on Investment in Selected Occupational Education Programs: Executive Summary." Rochester, N.Y.: Center of Governmental Research. ED 246 938. 9 pp. MF–$1.07; PC–$3.85.

Mingle, James R. 1986. "Assessment and the Variety of Its Forms." A Report Prepared for the Task Force on Planning and Quality Assessment of the South Carolina Commission on Higher Education. ED 279 226. 23 pp. MF–$1.07; PC–$3.85.

Mitchell, James V., Jr., ed. 1985. *The Ninth Mental Measurements Yearbook*. Lincoln, Neb.: University of Nebraska–Lincoln, Buros Institute of Mental Measurements.

Moran, T. Kenneth. 1987. "Research and Managerial Strategies for

Integrating Evaluation Research into Agency Decision Making." *Evaluation Review* 11: 612–30.
Munitz, Barry A., and Wright, Douglas J. 1980. "Institutional Approaches to Academic Program Evaluation." In *Academic Program Evaluation*, edited by Eugene Craver. New Directions for Institutional Research No. 27. San Francisco: Jossey-Bass.
National Governors Association. 1986. *Time for Results: The Governors' 1991 Report on Education*. Washington, D.C.: Author.
———. 1987. *The Governors' 1991 Report on Education: Results in Education, 1987.* Washington, D.C.: Author.
Nelsen, Edward A. 1985. "Review of NTE Programs." In *The Ninth Mental Measurements Yearbook*, edited by James V. Mitchell, Jr. Lincoln, Neb.: University of Nebraska–Lincoln, Buros Institute of Mental Measurements.
Northeast Missouri State University. 1984. *In Pursuit of Degrees of Integrity: A Value-Added Approach to Undergraduate Assessment*. Washington, D.C.: American Association of State Colleges and Universities.
Oppenheim, Don B. 1985. "Review of Pre-Professional Skills Test." In *The Ninth Mental Measurements Yearbook*, edited by James V. Mitchell, Jr. Lincoln, Neb.: University of Nebraska–Lincoln, Buros Institute of Mental Measurements.
Ory, John C. 1985. "Review of Stanford Test of Academic Skills (1982 Edition)." In *The Ninth Mental Measurements Yearbook*, edited by James V. Mitchell, Jr. Lincoln, Neb.: University of Nebraska–Lincoln, Buros Institute of Mental Measurements.
Pace, C. Robert. 1979. *Measuring Outcomes of College: 50 Years of Findings and Recommendations for the Future*. San Francisco: Jossey-Bass.
Palola, Ernest. 1981. "Multiple Perspectives, Multiple Channels." In *Increasing the Utilization of Institutional Research*, edited by Jack Lindquist. New Directions for Institutional Research No. 32. San Francisco: Jossey-Bass.
Palola, Ernest G., and Lehmann, T. 1976. "Improving Student Outcomes and Institutional Decision Making with PERC." In *Improving Educational Outcomes*, edited by Oscar T. Lenning. New Directions for Higher Education No. 16. San Francisco: Jossey-Bass.
Pascarella, Ernest T. 1987. "Are Value-Added Analyses Valuable?" In *Assessing the Outcomes of Higher Education*. Proceedings of the 1986 ETS Invitational Conference. Princeton, N.J.: Educational Testing Service.
Patton, M.; Grimes, P.; Guthrie, K.; Brennan, N.; French, B.; and Blyth, D. 1977. "In Search of Impact: An Analysis of the Utilization of Federal Health Evaluation Research." In *Using Social*

Research in Public Policy Making, edited by Carol Weiss. Lexington, Mass.: Lexington Books.

Polloway, Edward. 1985. "Review of Writing Proficiency Program." In *The Ninth Mental Measurements Yearbook*, edited by James V. Mitchell, Jr. Lincoln, Neb.: University of Nebraska–Lincoln, Buros Institute of Mental Measurements.

Project on Redefining the Meaning and Scope of Baccalaureate Degrees. 1985. *Integrity in the College Curriculum: A Report to the Academic Community*. Washington, D.C.: Association of American Colleges.

Quellmalz, Edys S. 1984. "Designing Writing Assessments: Balancing Fairness, Utility, and Cost." *Educational Evaluation and Policy Analysis* 6: 63–72.

———. 1985. "Review of Pre-Professional Skills Test." In *The Ninth Mental Measurements Yearbook*, edited by James V. Mitchell, Jr. Lincoln, Neb.: University of Nebraska–Lincoln, Buros Institute of Mental Measurements.

Roberts-Gray, Cynthia; Buller, Ann; and Sparkman, Alexa. 1987. "Linking Data with Action: Procedures for Developing Recommendations." *Evaluation Review* 11: 678–84.

Rossi, P.H., and Freeman, H.E. 1982. *Evaluation: A Systematic Approach*. 2d ed. Beverly Hills, Cal.: Sage Publishers.

Scannell, Dale P. 1985a. "Review of College Board English Composition Test with Essay." In *The Ninth Mental Measurements Yearbook*, edited by James V. Mitchell, Jr. Lincoln, Neb.: University of Nebraska–Lincoln, Buros Institute of Mental Measurements.

———. 1985b. "Review of NTE Programs." In *The Ninth Mental Measurements Yearbook*, edited by James V. Mitchell, Jr. Lincoln, Neb.: University of Nebraska–Lincoln, Buros Institute of Mental Measurements.

Scriven, Michael S. 1983. "Evaluation Ideologies." In *Evaluation Models: Viewpoints on Educational and Human Services Evaluation*, edited by George F. Madaus, Michael S. Scriven, and Daniel L. Stufflebeam. Boston: Kluwer Academic Publishers.

Shanahan, Timothy. 1985. "Review of Sequential Tests of Educational Progress, Series III." In *The Ninth Mental Measurements Yearbook*, edited by James V. Mitchell, Jr. Lincoln, Neb.: University of Nebraska–Lincoln, Buros Institute of Mental Measurements.

Siegel, Karolynn, and Tucker, P. June 1985. "The Utilization of Evaluation Research: A Case Analysis." *Evaluation Review* 9: 307–28.

Solmon, Lewis C. 1973. "The Definition and Impact of College Quality." In *Does College Matter? Some Evidence on the Impacts of Higher Education*, edited by Lewis C. Solmon and Paul J. Taubman. New York: Academic Press.

Study Group on the Conditions of Excellence in American Higher Education. 1984. *Involvement in Learning: Realizing the Potential of American Higher Education*. Washington, D.C.: National Institute of Education. ED 246 833. 127 pp. MF–$1.07; PC–$14.01.

Sweetland, Richard C., and Keyser, Daniel J., eds. 1983. *Tests: A Comprehensive Reference for Assessments in Psychology, Education, and Business.* Kansas City, Mo.: Test Corporation of America.

———, eds. 1986. *Tests: A Comprehensive Reference for Assessments in Psychology, Education, and Business*. 2d ed. Kansas City, Mo.: Test Corporation of America.

Sylvia, Ronald D.; Meier, Kenneth J.; and Gunn, Elizabeth M. 1985. *Program Planning and Evaluation for the Public Manager*. Monterey, Cal.: Brooks/Cole Publishing Co.

Taylor, Terry. 1985. "A Value-Added Student Assessment Model: Northeast Missouri State University." *Assessment and Evaluation in Higher Education* 10: 190–202.

Tierney, Robert J. 1985. "Review of Nelson-Denny Reading Test, Forms E and F." In *The Ninth Mental Measurements Yearbook*, edited by James V. Mitchell, Jr. Lincoln, Neb.: University of Nebraska–Lincoln, Buros Institute of Mental Measurements.

Van Meter, B.J., and Herrmann, B.A. Winter 1986–87. "Use and Misuse of the Nelson-Denny Reading Test." *Community College Review* 14: 25–30.

Wallace, Wimburn L. 1978. "College-Level Examination Program." In *The Eighth Mental Measurements Yearbook*, edited by Oscar K. Buros. Highland Park, N. J.: Gryphon Press.

Weick, Karl. 1979. *The Social Psychology of Organizing*. Reading, Mass.: Addison-Wesley.

Weiss, Carol H. 1988. "Evaluation for Decisions: Is Anybody There? Does Anybody Care?" *Evaluation Practice* 9: 5–19.

Weiss, Carol H., and Bucuvalas, Michael J. 1977. "The Challenge of Social Research to Decision Making." In *Using Social Research in Public Policy Making*, edited by Carol H. Weiss. Lexington, Mass.: Lexington Books.

———. 1980. *Social Science Research and Decision Making.* New York: Columbia University Press.

Willingham, Warren W. 1965. "Miller Analogies Test." A review in *The Sixth Mental Measurements Yearbook*, edited by Oscar K. Buros. Highland Park, N. J.: Gryphon Press.

Woehlke, Paula L. 1987. "Watson-Glaser Critical Thinking

Appraisal." In *Test Critiques,* edited by Daniel J. Keyser and Richard C. Sweetland. Kansas City, Mo.: Test Corporation of America.

Ysseldyke, James E. 1985. "Review of Nelson-Denny Reading Test, Forms E and F." In *The Ninth Mental Measurements Yearbook*, edited by James V. Mitchell, Jr. Lincoln, Neb.: University of Nebraska–Lincoln, Buros Institute of Mental Measurements.

INDEX

D

E

F

G

H

I

K

L

O

P

Q

T

ASHE-ERIC HIGHER EDUCATION REPORTS

Since 1983, the Association for the Study of Higher Education (ASHE) and the ERIC Clearinghouse on Higher Education at the George Washington University have cosponsored the ASHE-ERIC Higher Education Report series. The 1987 series is the sixteenth overall, with the American Association for Higher Education having served as cosponsor before 1983.

Each monograph is the definitive analysis of a tough higher education problem, based on thorough research of pertinent literature and institutional experiences. After topics are identified by a national survey, noted practitioners and scholars write the reports, with experts reviewing each manuscript before publication.

Eight monographs (10 monographs before 1985) in the ASHE-ERIC Higher Education Report series are published each year, available individually or by subscription. Subscription to eight issues is $60 regular; $50 for members of AERA, AAHE, and AIR; $40 for members of ASHE (add $10.00 for postage outside the United States).

Prices for single copies, including 4th class postage and handling, are $10.00 regular and $7.50 for members of AERA, AAHE, AIR, and ASHE ($7.50 regular and $6.00 for members for 1983 and 1984 reports, $6.50 regular and $5.00 for members for reports published before 1983). If faster UPS service is desired for U.S. and Canadian orders, add $1.00 for each publication ordered; overseas, add $5.00. For VISA and MasterCard payments, include card number, expiration date, and signature. Orders under $25 must be prepaid. Bulk discounts are available on orders of 15 or more reports (not applicable to subscriptions). Order from the Publications Department, ASHE-ERIC Higher Education Reports, the George Washington University, One Dupont Circle, Suite 630, Washington, D.C. 20036-1183, or phone us at 202/296-2597. Write for a publication list of all the Higher Education Reports available.

1987 ASHE-ERIC Higher Education Reports

1. Incentive Early Retirement Programs for Faculty: Innovative Responses to a Changing Environment
   Jay L. Chronister and Thomas R. Kepple, Jr.
2. Working Effectively with Trustees: Building Cooperative Campus Leadership
   Barbara E. Taylor
3. Formal Recognition of Employer-Sponsored Instruction: Conflict and Collegiality in Postsecondary Education
   Nancy S. Nash and Elizabeth M. Hawthorne
4. Learning Styles: Implications for Improving Educational Practices
   Charles S. Claxton and Patricia H. Murrell
5. Higher Education Leadership: Enhancing Skills through Professional Development Programs
   Sharon A. McDade
6. Higher Education and the Public Trust: Improving Stature in Colleges and Universities
   Richard L. Alfred and Julie Weissman
7. College Student Outcomes Assessment: A Talent Development Perspective
   Maryann Jacobi, Alexander Astin, and Frank Ayala, Jr.

1986 ASHE-ERIC Higher Education Reports

1. Post-tenure Faculty Evaluation: Threat or Opportunity?
   Christine M. Licata
2. Blue Ribbon Commissions and Higher Education: Changing Academe from the Outside
   Janet R. Johnson and Lawrence R. Marcus
3. Responsive Professional Education: Balancing Outcomes and Opportunities
   Joan S. Stark, Malcolm A. Lowther, and Bonnie M.K. Hagerty
4. Increasing Students' Learning: A Faculty Guide to Reducing Stress among Students
   Neal A. Whitman, David C. Spendlove, and Claire H. Clark
5. Student Financial Aid and Women: Equity Dilemma?
   Mary Moran
6. The Master's Degree: Tradition, Diversity, Innovation
   Judith S. Glazer
7. The College, the Constitution, and the Consumer Student: Implications for Policy and Practice
   Robert M. Hendrickson and Annette Gibbs
8. Selecting College and University Personnel: The Quest and the Questions
   Richard A. Kaplowitz

1985 ASHE-ERIC Higher Education Reports

1. Flexibility in Academic Staffing: Effective Policies and Practices
   Kenneth P. Mortimer, Marque Bagshaw, and Andrew T. Masland
2. Associations in Action: The Washington, D.C., Higher Education Community
   Harland G. Bloland
3. And on the Seventh Day: Faculty Consulting and Supplemental Income
   Carol M. Boyer and Darrell R. Lewis
4. Faculty Research Performance: Lessons from the Sciences and Social Sciences
   John W. Creswell
5. Academic Program Reviews: Institutional Approaches, Expectations, and Controversies
   Clifton F. Conrad and Richard F. Wilson
6. Students in Urban Settings: Achieving the Baccalaureate Degree
   Richard C. Richardson, Jr., and Louis W. Bender
7. Serving More Than Students: A Critical Need for College Student Personnel Services
   Peter H. Garland
8. Faculty Participation in Decision Making: Necessity or Luxury?
   Carol E. Floyd

1984 ASHE-ERIC Higher Education Reports

1. Adult Learning: State Policies and Institutional Practices
   K. Patricia Cross and Anne-Marie McCartan

2. Student Stress: Effects and Solutions
Neal A. Whitman, David C. Spendlove, and Claire H. Clark
3. Part-time Faculty: Higher Education at a Crossroads
Judith M. Gappa
4. Sex Discrimination Law in Higher Education: The Lessons of the Past Decade
J. Ralph Lindgren, Patti T. Ota, Perry A. Zirkel, and Nan Van Gieson
5. Faculty Freedoms and Institutional Accountability: Interactions and Conflicts
Steven G. Olswang and Barbara A. Lee
6. The High-Technology Connection: Academic/Industrial Cooperation for Economic Growth
Lynn G. Johnson
7. Employee Educational Programs: Implications for Industry and Higher Education
Suzanne W. Morse
8. Academic Libraries: The Changing Knowledge Centers of Colleges and Universities
Barbara B. Moran
9. Futures Research and the Strategic Planning Process: Implications for Higher Education
James L. Morrison, William L. Renfro, and Wayne I. Boucher
10. Faculty Workload: Research, Theory, and Interpretation
Harold E. Yuker

1983 ASHE-ERIC Higher Education Reports

1. The Path to Excellence: Quality Assurance in Higher Education
Laurence R. Marcus, Anita O. Leone, and Edward D. Goldberg
2. Faculty Recruitment, Retention, and Fair Employment: Obligations and Opportunities
John S. Waggaman
3. Meeting the Challenges: Developing Faculty Careers*
Michael C.T. Brookes and Katherine L. German
4. Raising Academic Standards: A Guide to Learning Improvement
Ruth Talbott Keimig
5. Serving Learners at a Distance: A Guide to Program Practices
Charles E. Feasley
6. Competence, Admissions, and Articulation: Returning to the Basics in Higher Education
Jean L. Preer
7. Public Service in Higher Education: Practices and Priorities
Patricia H. Crosson
8. Academic Employment and Retrenchment: Judicial Review and Administrative Action
Robert M. Hendrickson and Barbara A. Lee

*Out-of-print. Available through EDRS.

Dear Educator,

I welcome the ASHE-ERIC monograph series. The series is a service to those who need brief but dependable analyses of key issues in higher education.

(Rev.) Theodore M. Hesburgh, C.S.C.
President Emeritus, University of Notre Dame

Order Form

Quantity | Amount

_______ Please enter my subscription to the 1987 ASHE-ERIC Higher Education Reports at $60.00, 25% off the cover price. _______

_______ Please enter my subscription to the 1988 ASHE-ERIC Higher Education Reports at $60.00. _______

_______ Outside U.S., add $10.00 for postage per series. _______

Individual reports are available at the following prices:
1985 and forward, $10.00 each.
1983 and 1984, $7.50 each.
1982 and back, $6.50 each.

Please send me the following reports:

_______ Report No. ____ (____________________) _______
_______ Report No. ____ (____________________) _______
_______ Report No. ____ (____________________) _______

SUBTOTAL: _______
Optional U.P.S. Shipping ($1.00 per book) _______
TOTAL AMOUNT DUE: _______

NOTE: All prices subject to change.

Name ____________________

Title ____________________

Institution ____________________

Address ____________________

____

City ____________ State ________ ZIP ________

Phone ____________________

Signature ____________________

☐ Check enclosed, payable to ASHE. ☐ Purchase order attached.
☐ Please charge my credit card:
☐ VISA ☐ MasterCard (check one)

☐☐☐☐☐☐☐☐☐☐☐☐☐☐☐☐

Expiration date ________

ASHE

ERIC®

Send to: ASHE-ERIC Higher Education Reports
The George Washington University
One Dupont Circle, Suite 630, Dept. G4
Washington, D.C. 20036-1183

NOTES

NOTES